My Home Among the Hills

There's a land of rolling mountains
Where the sky is blue above;
And though I may roam I hurry home
To the friendly hills I love.

Where the moonlit meadows ring with the call of
 whip-poor-wills,
Always you will find me in my home among the hills.
And where the sun draws rainbows in the mist of
 waterfalls and mountain rills,
My heart will be always in the West Virginia hills.

There autumn hillsides are bright with scarlet trees
And in the spring the robins sing while apple
 blossoms whisper in the breeze
And there is music in the flashing streams, and joy in
 fields of daffodils.
Laughter through the happy valleys of my home
 among the hills.

—E. W. "Bill" James (Hon. 1973)
 Trustee, 1965–1978

OUR HOME
Among The Hills

West Virginia Wesleyan College's First 125 Years

OUR HOME
Among The Hills

West Virginia Wesleyan College's First 125 Years

Brett T. Miller

Unless otherwise noted, all images are from collections of the West Virginia Wesleyan College Archives or were taken by staff members of Wesleyan's Office of Advancement. A year in parentheses following a name indicates the year of graduation from West Virginia Wesleyan College.

Copyright © 2014 by West Virginia Wesleyan College

The Donning Company Publishers
184 Business Park Drive, Suite 206
Virginia Beach, VA 23462

Steve Mull, General Manager
Barbara Buchanan, Office Manager
Anne Burns, Editor
Rick Boley, Graphic Designer
Kathy Adams, Imaging Artist
Sherry Hartman, Project Research Coordinator
Nathan Stufflebean, Research and Marketing Supervisor
Katie Gardner, Marketing Advisor
George Nikolovski, Project Director

Cataloging-in-Publication Data available from the Library of Congress
    ISBN: 978-1-57864-907-5

Printed in the United States of America at Walsworth Publishing Company

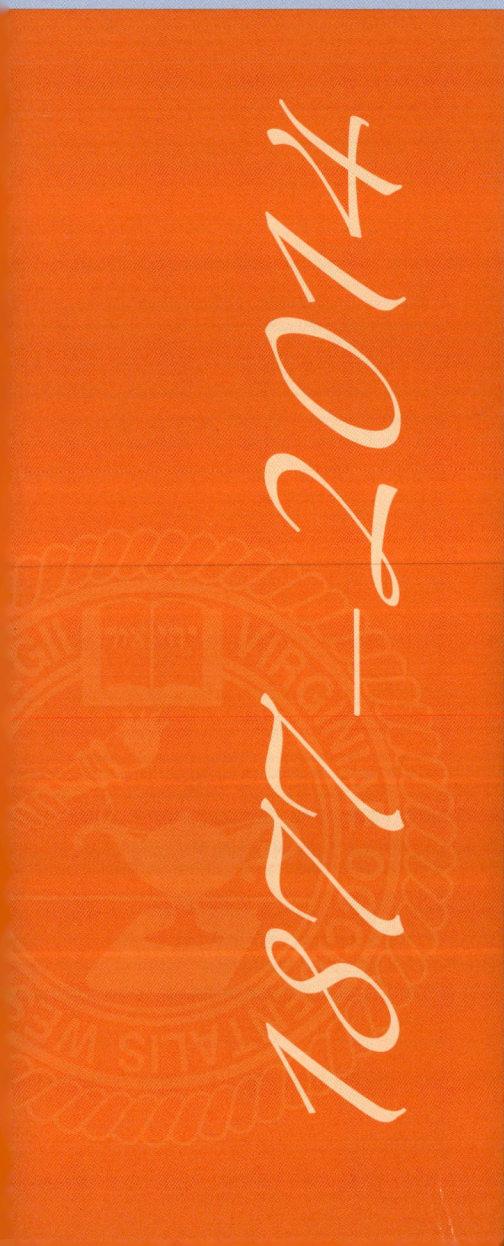

1877–2014

TABLE OF CONTENTS

Preface

The task of writing this history of West Virginia Wesleyan College has been both a great joy and an immense challenge. The joy has come through the opportunity over the past months to explore Wesleyan's story in great depth and to revel in its complexity and richness. Uncovering unique facts and wonderful photographs revealed Wesleyan in a way that few have the opportunity to see beyond a few fleeting student years. Still, it is undeniable that this special place known as West Virginia Wesleyan College has a profound impact on almost everyone who enters its portals, regardless of how long they remain. At the heart of West Virginia Wesleyan College are the committed people—founders, students, faculty, administrators, staff, alumni, trustees, friends—who have come together over the course of 125 years in the pursuit of the shared enterprise of education. It is their story I fervently hope is reflected in this publication.

The challenge of writing a text like this is the reality that, because so many people have worked to make the institution successful, any attempt to name them all would invariably fail. We look to history so we can "see ourselves" and, inevitably, some may not see themselves in this book. An attempt has been made to balance the diverse facets of college life, the traditions that make Wesleyan unique, and the administrative history that has shaped the course of the institution. Wesleyan is fortunate to have two published histories by Thomas Haught (Sem. 1894; Hon. 1916) in 1940 and Kenneth Plummer in 1965. These extraordinarily detailed works provided the foundation for this book's first two chapters and are invaluable for their early insights.

It is a pleasure to recognize those individuals who supported this publication and saw it to completion. President Pamela Balch (1971) and Vice Presidents Bob Skinner (1975), Barry Pritts, and Boyd Creasman deserve thanks for their institutional support of the project. The members of the 125th Anniversary Advisory Committee have been invaluable in helping to keep the project on track and on time. To the staff of the Annie Merner Pfeiffer Library—Paula McGrew (1978), Beth Rogers (1997), Sue Roth (1985), Carol Bowman (1992), Carol Smith (1990), Rhonda Bennett (1993), Jennifer Rinker, and Wilma Whitlock—I am grateful for your patience, helpfulness, and support through what I am sure has been as long and trying a period for you as it has been for me. Amy Tenney and Noel Tenney (1979) of the Upshur County Historical Society deserve mention for their research assistance and help in locating photographs. Finally, to those who read and commented on the manuscript—Beth Rogers (1997), Barbara Morrissette, Kristi Lawrence Wilkerson (1999), and Kenneth Welliver—your input made the text much stronger than it ever could have been on its own. Your good work is more appreciated than you know.

CHAPTER 1

From Seminary to University to College

The story of West Virginia Wesleyan College begins long before the school itself was even an idea in the minds of its founders. Education in western Virginia through the early- and mid-nineteenth century was inconsistent, reflecting the frontier lifestyle of the area's earliest settlers. Organized schools often provided limited education, usually only to the eighth grade. To compound matters, education outside the home was often available only to those with the financial means to pay tuition and boarding costs. Churches viewed education as a natural extension of their ministry, and the Methodist Episcopal Church attempted a number of times to establish educational institutions prior to the Civil War and West Virginia's statehood in 1863. One example, the Mt. Hebron School in Cabell County, came under state control in 1838 and eventually became the Marshall Academy (later Marshall College).[1]

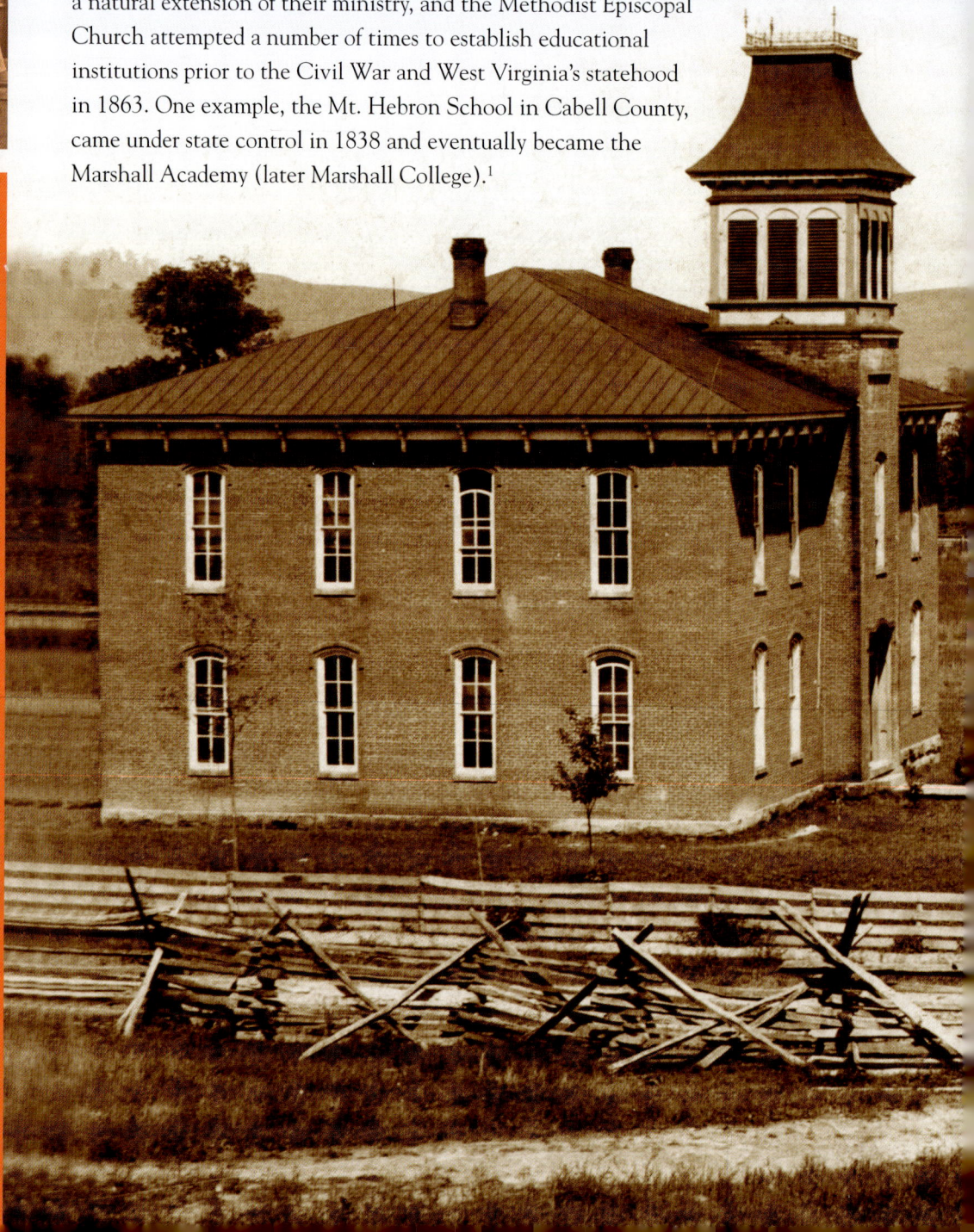

1877–1930

Because of the Methodist Conference's difficulties sustaining a school, many families looked to the state university in Morgantown (now West Virginia University, founded in 1867). The university's earliest administrators were Methodist and the church felt it had some degree of influence over the course of the school. When a non-Methodist president was elected in 1882 and the curriculum of the University of Virginia was adopted, the church felt it had effectively lost control of the institution.[2] To stem the tide of Methodist students seeking education elsewhere, the conference formed a committee on education in 1874 and began advocating for the creation of a Methodist Conference seminary to be located within the state. Unlike contemporary seminaries which specialize in graduate theological education, seminaries of the late 1800s were generally residential schools that provided the equivalent of secondary or college preparatory education.

Little progress was made between 1874 and 1876, though the committee received an unsolicited proposal from the town of Buckhannon in 1877, supported by a pledge of $8,090 and a three-acre plot of land to construct the school building. For unknown reasons, the conference did not act concretely on the Buckhannon proposal, but appointed trustees for the West Virginia Conference Seminary in 1878 that were authorized to receive proposals and gifts and to negotiate construction.[3]

Buckhannon's desire for an educational institution was not without precedent, as the Presbyterians had made an ill-timed attempt to found a school called the Baxter Institute in 1861 on a site near Wesleyan's present-day campus. Land was set aside and lumber was already at the construction site when General

Looking down College Avenue between 1890 and 1895, the Seminary Building is to the right and the Buckhannon Normal and Classical Academy, a United Brethren in Christ preparatory school which closed in 1897, is on the left. (Photo courtesy of the Upshur County Historical Society)

The Baltimore and Ohio Railroad was one of the few ways to reach Buckhannon easily. The #7 train, seen here around 1915 at the depot on North Kanawha Street, made five daily trips north to Tygart Junction in Barbour County, West Virginia. (Photo courtesy of the Upshur County Historical Society)

McClellan's army invaded Upshur County during the Civil War, raiding the supplies for fires and other purposes. It took until 1905 for the Presbyterian Church to receive restitution of $1,431 from the government.[4]

An offering in 1884 to build up the seminary endowment was proposed and, according to Thomas Haught's 1940 history of Wesleyan, a resolution passed by the Methodist Conference in 1885 put it on record as against any future attempt to revive the Northwestern Virginia Academy in Clarksburg, another early Methodist school.[5] The academy opened in the fall 1843 and operated successfully until the outbreak of the Civil War caused its closure in 1862. Reopened in 1865, the school never regained its former momentum and the withdrawal of conference support shifted valuable energy and resources to the seminary in Buckhannon.

An expanded board of trustees was authorized to find a location for the school in 1886 and received proposals from Wheeling, Kingwood, Grafton, Salem, Parkersburg, Clarksburg, Philippi, Weston, and, again, Buckhannon. Haught points out the board's final selection of Buckhannon was unintentionally fraught with superstitious symbolism:

It is interesting to note that there were thirteen of the sixteen members of the board present at this meeting on the thirteenth of July and that on the thirteenth ballot of the next day's session they reached the decision to locate the Seminary in Buckhannon. What a bone for both friends and hecklers! The former will see in this unwitting challenge to the superstition of unlucky numerals a forecast of the school's most wholesome growth… the latter will ascribe all the calamities that express to them the difference between what is, and what might have been, in the life of the school, to the blindness of the well-meaning founders who failed to see the hand of the fates writing in triplicate this omen of their displeasure.[6]

The trustees immediately set about finding a suitable plot upon which to establish a school. On July 15, 1887, the trustees approved an offer by Wilbur F. and Daniel Carper for sixty acres

The earliest known photograph of the Seminary Building shows the final stages of construction in 1890.

Bennett Hutchinson, a thirty-one-year-old Methodist minister serving a church in Rhode Island, enjoyed a $1,200 salary as the seminary's first president.

across the river from Wesleyan's current campus. Concerns quickly arose about the feasibility of the Carper site, specifically the need to build a suitable bridge to connect to Buckhannon city proper. In August 1887, the board asked to be released from its option to purchase the Carper property and instead accepted a forty-three-acre plot from Levi Leonard. Included in the agreement was a provision that clay and mud from the site could be used to make bricks for the seminary building, an ideal scenario considering the easy access to water needed for the process from the Buckhannon River.

A school building became the next priority. A contract was awarded in October 1888 for the construction of a three-story brick and stone building on the highest point of the generally empty campus. Bennett Hutchinson was elected president in June 1890 and immediately set to work hiring faculty, advertising the school, and procuring furnishings for the new building. The faculty in the first year included Hutchinson and Frank Trotter, who later served as vice president and acting president of the seminary and went on to become a dean and acting president at West Virginia University.

The West Virginia Conference Seminary officially opened on September 3, 1890, and Roy Reger (Sem. 1893) became the first of seventy students to sign the registration book. Tuition for a full year cost $25 and the first year's enrollment totaled 201 students. According to future faculty member, dean, and three-time acting president Thomas Haught (Sem. 1894), there were only six faculty members in place by the end of the first school year.[7] Families in Buckhannon boarded many students in their homes and saw to their physical, educational, and spiritual well-being. Boarding with unauthorized individuals in Buckhannon or in local hotels was forbidden, and a list of approved homes was kept in the president's office. Students were also discouraged from boarding near Main Street to avoid distractions to regular study.[8] The catalog describes Buckhannon as:

…almost an ideal location for an institution of learning. Hardly another town in West Virginia has a natural site equal in beauty and attractiveness. It is situated on the uplands about 1300 feet above sea level, near the center of the State, and railroads are already finished or being built to almost every section of the State. The town is healthful, well supplied with churches, HAS NEVER HAD A LIQUOR SALOON, and is probably as nearly free from evil influences as any town of its size in the country. The people are intelligent and hospitable, and are ready to extend a cordial welcome to our students.[9]

Below: Literary society programs, often judged by a panel, consisted of oration, musical performances, mock trials, debates, and sometimes more elaborate theatrical productions.

Above: Tongue-in-cheek, these senior women of the Chrestomathean and Excelsior Literary Societies in September 1897, who dubbed themselves "The Seven Widows," lament that the "boys" are only paying attention to the "new girls."

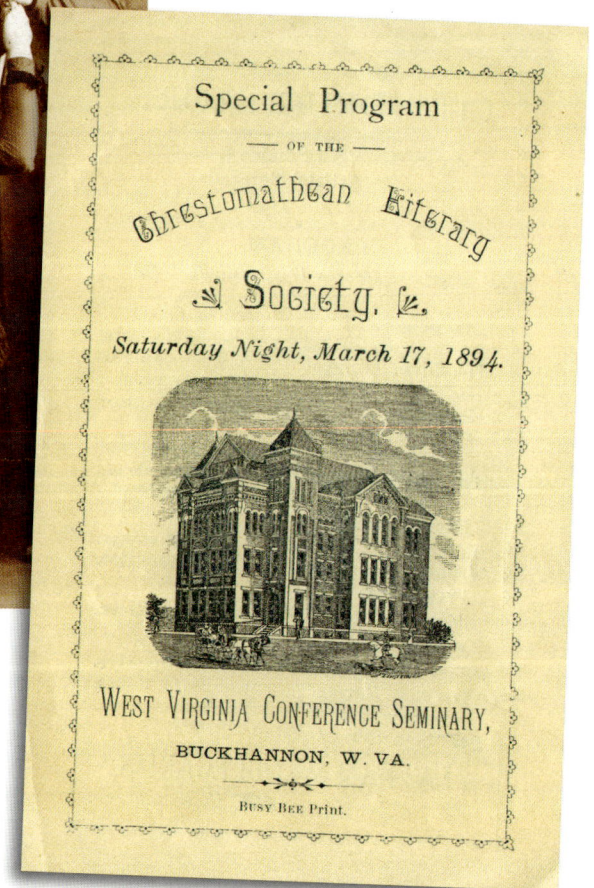

Special Program

— OF THE —

Chrestomathean Literary

Society.

Saturday Night, March 17, 1894.

WEST VIRGINIA CONFERENCE SEMINARY,

BUCKHANNON, W. VA.

Busy Bee Print.

Recognizing at the outset that cultural opportunities would be scarce and a vibrant atmosphere for learning would require the involvement of all students, two literary societies were established by President Hutchinson, named Chrestomathean and Excelsior. Each society had a large assembly hall set aside for it in the Seminary Building and all students were assigned randomly to one society or the other when they arrived. Officers were elected annually. These organizations, common in many schools of the time, served as a combined social, intellectual, and musical outlet for students.

In today's terms campus and residence life would easily be considered austere and rules regarding conduct strict. At 7:00 p.m. the seminary bell was rung, indicating to all students it was time to return to their rooms or boarding houses for quiet study. To maintain the religious emphasis of the school, students were not only required to attend daily chapel services, but were also expected to attend a church of their preference on Sunday mornings. Students were forbidden to use tobacco in any form and were similarly forbidden to loiter in front of stores, on streets, or in public places. Even recreational

The seminary's small library was acquired mostly through donations of Methodist ministers and supporters of the fledgling school.

Men gather on the steps of the Seminary Building (background) and on the porch of Ladies Hall (foreground), while women appear from open windows in this late 1890s view of campus. The fence was intended to keep local farm animals from roaming onto the grounds.

AGNES HOWARD AND AGNES HOWARD HALL

Designed by architect M. F. Geisey of Wheeling, West Virginia, and known as "Ladies Hall" from its opening in 1895, the first residence hall on campus was meant to house sixty students, but was quickly pressed into housing seventy. It contained a kitchen, dining room, parlor, and a bathroom on each floor. Water was supplied to the building by a windmill pump that sent water to a tank in the attic. Electricity was added to the building shortly after it was constructed, though spotty service led to frequent failures. The building was named Agnes Howard Hall in 1920 in memory of the Wesleyan student (pictured far left) from Cowen, West Virginia, who died tragically after her freshman year in 1917 from rheumatoid arthritis. The building also honored Agnes's father, C. D. Howard, who was a trustee and substantial benefactor of the college.

outings were restricted without approval, and any student wishing to leave town or separate from the institution was required to secure permission of the president.

Through the 1970s, freshmen had to identify themselves by wearing beanies during the first part of the school year. Older students could also ask freshmen to recite college cheers or songs.

Haught points out that, while the seminary provided the equivalent of a secondary education, most students were closer in age to traditional college students and were generally more mature.[10] Many students already served as teachers in local schools and were enrolled in the normal course of study to achieve state teacher certification. The seminary schedule was arranged into three terms: fall (ten weeks), winter (fourteen weeks), and spring (fourteen weeks). The public school calendar was typically only sixteen weeks in the winter, meaning schoolteachers could attend the fall term, teach during the winter term, arrange spring courses by correspondence, and arrive on campus only two weeks into the spring term. Students not academically prepared for the seminary course could enroll in a two-year remedial/preparatory course, though it was recommended students under the age of fourteen not apply.

It quickly became apparent that in order to sustain the momentum of the initial years and attract new students, a women's dormitory would be essential. An existing $20,000 debt incurred from construction of the Seminary Building had to be addressed, and a concerted fundraising effort through 1894 allowed the trustees to begin the $25,000 construction of "Ladies Hall" in 1895. Despite enthusiastic supporters in Buckhannon and elsewhere, finances were a chronic issue for the young seminary. President Hutchinson exemplified the spirit of sacrifice that characterized the early days of the school by personally paying to construct a residence for himself near the Oak Grove at the intersection of Sedgwick Street and College Avenue in 1892. His only stipulation was that the board purchase the property from him when his relationship with the college ended. Four more presidents lived in the house until it became a residence for female students in 1922 and was later demolished in the spring of 1952.

Dinner was served to female students in the Ladies Hall dining room, while male students took meals in their host homes or in boarding clubs in Buckhannon.

With so much emphasis placed on the educational and religious development of students, athletics were slow to develop at the seminary. The Department of Physical Culture constituted the only sanctioned physical activity for students and consisted mostly of army drill. This changed in November 1899 when a group of Wesleyan students led by Henry White, a former West Virginia University player, challenged a group of civil engineers working on the B&O Railroad to a game of football. The sport itself was just starting to come to prominence around the country and the seminary team, aside from White, consisted entirely of players without previous experience. Future army chaplain Colonel Frank Thompson (Sem. 1902) was elected team captain. Despite curiosity about the sport, attendance was small due to cold temperatures, and the result of the game was

Pick-up baseball games, such as this one photographed between 1902 and 1905, were a common form of student entertainment before football became more prominent.

Frank Thompson (Sem. 1902), captain of the first football team, idolized the Poe brothers of Princeton University, who wore orange and black turtleneck sweaters during football games. Thompson declared that the 1899 seminary team, seen here, would do likewise, establishing Wesleyan's school colors.

Simon Boyers's term as president was the second shortest in the institution's history, after which he returned to the Methodist pastorate in Ohio.

disappointing to those who stayed to the end. No touchdowns were scored, and a scuffle ensued over whether a safety scored by the engineers was legitimate, eventually resulting in a declared draw. Despite the lackluster first game, football became an eagerly anticipated staple of the college's early years.[11]

President Hutchinson's fruitful and stable administration of the West Virginia Conference Seminary ended at the conclusion of the 1897–1898 winter term, and Frank Trotter assumed the duties of acting president until Simon L. Boyers was elected in June 1898. Though described as "a gentleman whose educational and cultural experience, pleasant appearance and Christian character seemed to fit him admirably for the job,"[12] some questionable decisions caused students and faculty to doubt Boyers's competency. As recounted by Haught:

In the spring of the year 1899 the President had almost the entire front part of the campus…planted with potatoes, in part, and the rest of the area sown in oats… The goal to be attained by farming the campus is not a matter of record…After threading their way through the growing potatoes and oats to attend class, it would have been no less than a miracle if the active brain of some farmer boy had not guided his hand in the use of a scythe on the eve of his departure at the end of the school year. In the darkness these lads seemed unable to distinguish the line demarcating the boundary between the oats and potatoes. One such young man, whose alibi for that night was not established beyond a doubt, was subjected to rather stern discipline by the President. Another…will tell you privately that he got rid of the temptation to swing the scythe on that occasion only by the time honored method of yielding to it.[13]

More trouble arose when Boyers, concerned over possible further vandalism, employed armed security guards to patrol campus in the nighttime hours. A student supposedly engaged in a Halloween prank was shot in the fall of 1899, leading to an investigation by the trustees and the threat of a lawsuit by the boy's father, who accused the "shotgun administration" of extreme negligence.[14] While the student survived his injuries and the president barely survived a vote by the board asking for his resignation, the damage was done. Boyers's short administration came to an end with his resignation on June 12, 1900.

The trustees again found themselves in search of a president and elected John Weir on June 28, 1900. The lack of an endowment was tackled immediately, with $100,000 raised by 1903 in conjunction with the Twentieth Century Thank Offering conducted by the Methodist Episcopal Church. Weir's enthusiasm for the school led to substantial private donations, including a $25,000 gift from Dr. D. K. Pearsons of Chicago. As was

John Weir, originally from Canada, came to Wesleyan in 1900 from Scio College in Ohio, where he was president.

W. O. Mills was a former principal of the Buckhannon Normal and Classical Academy and taught mathematics and engineering at the seminary after the academy closed. He is seen here around 1901 with engineering students.

The staff of the 1906 college newspaper, the *Pharos*, included future Wesleyan president Roy McCuskey, seated at the table to the left.

common practice in the early years of the school, seminary classes would name themselves after an influential professor (the W. O. Mills Class of 1902) or, in this case, a substantial benefactor (Pearsons Class of 1904).

Student activities through the turn of the century continued to diversify. Bennett

Hutchinson began a newspaper called the *Seminary Herald* in 1893 to communicate with donors and alumni, but it wasn't until around 1899 that it became a student publication. The *Seminary Collegiate*, as it became known, contained student writings and orations, alumni updates, and campus news. The *Collegiate* was published until the fall of 1904 when its name changed to the *Pharos* upon suggestion of Professor W. O. Mills. The first yearbook, the *Murmurmontis*, was published in 1904 and took its name from a suggestion by Latin professor Frank Trotter. The word roughly translates to "voice of the mountains."[15]

When the campus was expanded again in 1902, the trustees opted for an entirely modest, yet functional three-story brick and stone building to serve as home for the seminary's Conservatory of Music. The Annex Building was constructed for $6,500 and put into use in January 1903. Despite its double-insulated walls

The Annex Building was constructed in 1902 for $6,500 and has served as home to numerous academic departments and campus offices.

SEMINARY BUILDING FIRE

The morning of Saturday, February 5, 1905, began like any other, with students gathering for classes in the Seminary Building (as was the schedule during those years). Temperatures to negative fifteen degrees the night before led the plant foreman to fire the coal boiler more generously that morning, and either a spark in the basement or poor pipe insulation started a fire, which traveled upward inside the walls. With lectures in progress, it took some time before smoke filled the hallways and flames appeared. Firefighters struggled to get water through frozen lines from the distant hydrant near Sedgwick Street. By mid-afternoon the building was deemed a complete loss, though nobody was killed or injured in the blaze. The seminary bell survived with only a small crack, despite falling four stories into burning debris in the basement. It was eventually hung in the Administration Building in 1906 and later moved to the steeple of Wesley Chapel.

Right: Classes were relocated to the Annex Building, the parlors of Ladies Hall, and various places around Buckhannon. As this placard posted in the aftermath of the fire indicates, no class time was lost.

Below: Students and faculty worked quickly to save furniture, school records, and library books, seen at the base of the building, often throwing them unceremoniously from windows.

Proclamation to Students

All students are requested to hold together and be ready for work Tuesday.

Necessary arrangements will be made to continue all classes without loss of time.

Respectfully,
FRANK B. TROTTER, Vice President.

for soundproofing, the "Music Box," as it was known at the time, was as much maligned for the sounds emanating from its studios as it was for its unassuming appearance. Yet little could the board have recognized at the time how fortuitous their seemingly "cheap" construction decision would be for the future survival of the institution.

The 1904 women's intramural basketball squad is identified with W.U.W.V. for Wesleyan University of West Virginia during Wesleyan's name change.

Fires were an all-too-common occurrence at the time, and many smaller schools did not recover from the loss of a building. Wesleyan proved a fortunate exception in the aftermath of the Seminary Building fire of 1905. President John Weir was in Charleston, West Virginia, when he received the news and rushed back to Buckhannon. Professor Frank Trotter took charge in his stead. The Annex Building, so criticized for its simplicity, was pressed into service well beyond its imagined capacity as classes were moved into its studios, as well as into the parlors of Ladies Hall, for the next year.

President Weir's idealism became a rallying point for the rebuilding of the seminary on its current site, despite a tempting offer of land and a pledge of financial support to relocate to Parkersburg, West Virginia. With quick assistance from around the state, and a sizeable gift from steel magnate and philanthropist Andrew Carnegie, the current Administration Building was ready for use in 1906. Having learned from the previous building's destruction, a new central heating plant for the campus was constructed away from the buildings. With its prominent smokestack often belching dark smoke, "Old Smokey" became a campus fixture until it was torn down in 1965 to make way for Wesley Chapel.

What also arguably kept the seminary in Buckhannon were major curricular developments in the years leading up to the fire. President Hutchinson recognized that West Virginia's improving

The first sundial was purchased in Baltimore, Maryland, by Dean William A. Haggerty and was installed in 1907. Seen here is the second sundial with professor Thomas Haught on the left. The fourth and current sundial was a gift of the graduating class of 2003.

educational system would render the seminary irrelevant unless it moved toward providing college-level programs. A first year of collegiate-level work was added in 1892, followed by a sophomore year in 1901. The final move from seminary to college came in 1903 when the board agreed to grant bachelor's degrees in three courses of study: humanities/classical, science, and literature. The enthusiasm for this new development was so great the administration proposed the conference seminary be renamed as the Wesleyan University of West Virginia, which was approved by the trustees in April 1904.

Because of the Seminary Building fire, commencement was held at the Buckhannon Opera House, where five students became the first college graduates in 1905. They also had the distinction of being the only graduates of Wesleyan University of West Virginia. Feeling the designation of "university" was too ambitious after all, the trustees orphaned the class by changing the school's name to West Virginia Wesleyan College two days prior to commencement in June 1906. This made the class of 1906 the second to graduate with degrees,

but the first to graduate from West Virginia Wesleyan College. The seminary course of study was shortened to three years and the name was changed to the preparatory department in 1906 and later to the academy in 1908. As the curriculum became better established and secondary education around West Virginia improved, the academy course became less necessary and was discontinued entirely in 1922.

After an eventful tenure, John Weir resigned in 1907 and the board continued its tradition of electing Methodist clergymen, choosing Carl Doney. Arriving in September,

Coming from a Methodist church in Washington, D.C., President Carl Gregg Doney encouraged many students, including future trustee chair Clyde O. Law (Sem. 1905; College 1909), to pursue further education beyond Wesleyan.

The observance of May Day, seen here in 1912, began as early as 1900 with music, a picnic, and the winding of the maypole. A queen of May was elected by the student body and was crowned during the festivities.

Christian and missionary student organizations, including the Homiletics Association, the YMCA, and the YWCA, seen here celebrating "All World Day" in 1912, flourished through the 1910s and 1920s.

Doney gained a reputation as a stern, but fair disciplinarian with a keen sense of public relations. As in his previous churches, Doney acquired a printing press for the college and trained students to use it to create fundraising and recruitment materials in exchange for tuition assistance. Along with the college's first official dean, William A. Haggerty, Doney continued the work started by President Weir to advance the burgeoning college program, including the change of class lengths from forty-five minutes to a full hour in 1909.

Doney's presidency also corresponds with what was arguably the golden age of men's athletics at Wesleyan. Construction of a gymnasium in 1912 prompted the rapid

expansion of basketball, and all-around athlete Harry A. Stansbury (Acad. 1909; College 1915) organized the first state high school basketball tournament at Wesleyan in 1914 while still a student. No such tournament previously existed and its leadership and organization were passed from student to student in a tradition that continued until the tournament moved to West Virginia University in 1938. The baseball team started around 1900 and won its first state championship in 1914, followed by two more in 1917 and 1920. The 1912 football team stands out from many others because of a recruitment trip around the state made by quarterback Harry A. Stansbury. An unheard of practice at the time, Stansbury's talent search yielded Wesleyan

football great and future Professional Football Hall of Fame inductee Alfred Earle "Greasy" Neale (Acad. 1914) as well as future Wesleyan football coach John Kellison (Acad. 1912; College 1916). The 1912 team went undefeated, including a 19-14 upset of West Virginia University on a trick play that won the game.

The science curriculum, present from nearly the beginning, grew substantially thanks to the generosity of Colonel Sydney Haymond and his wife, Virginia. Both served as trustees, with Virginia filling her husband's seat upon his death in 1912. Science courses were taught in the Administration Building until Virginia Haymond made a substantial gift to construct a new science building as a memorial to her husband. The

Constructed in 1912 for $10,000 and expanded in 1920, the gymnasium contained a small swimming pool, offices, and classrooms in addition to the main basketball court.

Students held a rally on the courthouse steps in 1913 to celebrate a second football victory against West Virginia University in as many years. A funeral carriage was even on hand (bottom right) to carry the "body" of WVU.

Under Coach John Felton, the undefeated 1912 football team handed opponents a number of lopsided defeats, including this 59-0 decision against Marshall College and a 103-0 trouncing of Davis and Elkins College.

building quickly became a tribute to both Haymonds for their dedication and service to Wesleyan. Virginia saw the building completed in 1914 and dedicated in 1916 before her death in 1917.

In 1914 the board granted President Doney a leave of absence to travel in Europe with his family for ten months. Archduke Franz Ferdinand was assassinated while the family was in Frankfurt, Germany, and they left England just as war was declared across the continent.[16] Despite the welcome respite from campus responsibilities, Doney resigned in 1915 to become the president of Willamette University. Before the year was up, the board turned to Wallace B. Fleming for leadership. Known as an excellent fundraiser, Fleming quickly initiated a $500,000 campaign in 1916 and completed some academic developments initiated during Doney's term. New programs were added in religion and

In the absence of any organized intercollegiate sports for women, a special physical culture curriculum was established prior to the addition of physical education courses for men. Seen here is a women's track and field meet between 1914 and 1918.

Bible in 1915 and in domestic and agricultural science in 1916 (which became home economics by 1919). Students could also obtain a master of arts degree by completing an additional forty-five hours of coursework in a major area and by writing a thesis. Sixteen students were granted graduate degrees between 1913 and 1935.

The United States entered World War I in 1917 and, as young men from around the country mobilized, Wesleyan became home to two hundred members of the government's Student Army Training Corps from October to December 1918. The gymnasium was converted into a barracks and dining facility as the men undertook combat training, drill, and academic coursework. The program was short-lived, as the armistice ended the war on November 11, 1918, and many of the student trainees were stricken with the virulent flu epidemic that circled the globe toward the war's end. Because the flu strain disproportionately affected young people, the college was particularly hard hit and at least one Wesleyan student died as a result. Students and cadets alike were quarantined during much of the fall and the Annex Building was pressed into service as a hospital facility.

Wallace Fleming left Wesleyan in 1922, and Elmer Guy Cutshall was chosen to succeed him in 1923. Cutshall found the college in a precarious financial position, with a large amount of pledged money from the 1916 fundraising campaign still uncollected. While his solution of raising tuition from $50 to $60 and to insist on tuition payment in advance was met with

President Wallace Fleming is credited with writing the college's alma mater around 1918, which is set to the tune of the famous sextet from Donizetti's opera *Lucia di Lammermoor*.

Members of the Student Army Training Corps arranged in front of the Administration Building just prior to departing campus in 1918.

some hesitancy on the part of the board, the canvassing effort Cutshall initiated to collect pledges was generally successful. All preparatory programs were phased out, so by the 1923–1924 school year only college-level work was offered. As the student body grew steadily through the 1920s, so too did the desire for more diverse student organizations; gone were the days when two literary societies could accommodate student interest. A small student government was formed in 1922, though its function was limited until it was expanded into Community Council in 1947.[17]

Despite generally positive developments, Cutshall's tenure lasted only two years. He spent a portion of that time recovering from a near-fatal bout of sepsis that developed after an accidental cut received at a barbershop.[18] A major development in student life came just after Cutshall's departure when the trustees officially permitted the formation of Greek letter organizations in October 1925. Sigma Delta Chi and Chi Alpha Tau became the first chartered sorority and fraternity on campus, respectively, though some unofficial Greek letter clubs existed prior to this.

Elmer Guy Cutshall was reported to be the youngest college president in the United States when he was elected in 1923 at age thirty-two.

Right: Students, like these gathered at local photographer Hode Clark's river camp in 1924, often enjoyed leisure activities such as canoeing on the Buckhannon River or weekend picnics.

Below: The exact origin of the college's mascot remains a mystery, though the first reference to "Bob Cats" came in 1922. Despite claims to the contrary, football coach Bob Higgins is likely the inspiration. Seen here is an "unofficial" mascot at a 1934 football game.

The institution's increasingly heavy focus on athletics led to problems when Homer Wark was elected president in 1926. Many alumni voiced concern that the college was not accredited and that this might affect the ability of graduates to secure jobs outside of West Virginia. Wesleyan's application to the North Central Association, the regional accrediting body, was denied because of the athletic department's practice of providing free room and board to athletes, as well as the heavy, uncontrolled debt accrued by the football program. After the 1926 football season, Wark proposed and the trustees agreed to eliminate two athletic staff positions and to restructure the way athletic aid was administered. While the reforms had modest effect and Wark still had to dismiss one football player who was playing professional football on Sundays, the corrections were enough to convince the North Central Association to grant Wesleyan accreditation in 1927.

While financial conditions weren't ideal, the shortage of campus housing for female students became a pressing concern. Architect Carl Reger (Sem. 1897) was engaged to design an addition to Agnes Howard Hall, and the new Meade Street wing was completed for occupancy in January 1929. Unfortunately, the stock market crash in October 1929 stymied the college's hopes for faster development. President Wark was forced to reduce his own salary by $1,000 that year and, sensing the coming crisis, attempted to resign in 1930. The board refused to accept and he continued as president until 1931. With accreditation, an expanded physical plant, and a growing student body, the college should have been poised for significant growth. Instead, it found itself at the doorstep of one of the darkest and most uncertain periods in its history.

Opposite: Homer Wark, a former professor at Boston University, resigned after his administration was increasingly hindered by the economic depression, which began in 1929.

WESLEYAN'S PRO FOOTBALL HALL OF FAME INDUCTEES

Wesleyan has the unique distinction of two Pro Football Hall of Fame inductees in Alfred Earle "Greasy" Neale (HOF class of 1969; pictured left) and Clifford "Gip" Battles (HOF class of 1968; pictured right). Both were all-around athletes at Wesleyan; Neale from 1912 to 1914 in football, basketball, and baseball, and Battles in football, baseball, basketball, track, and tennis from 1928 to 1932. Neale coached at Wesleyan while also playing professional baseball for the Cincinnati Reds (which included a World Series win in 1919). He later coached the Washington & Jefferson College football team to a Rose Bowl victory in 1922 and coached the Philadelphia Eagles to national championships in 1948 and 1949. Battles distinguished himself as a player on the Boston Braves (later the Boston Redskins and then the Washington Redskins) from 1932 to 1937, becoming the first player to rush for more than 200 yards in a game in 1933 and winning a NFL championship in 1937. A salary dispute ended his professional playing career in 1937, though he went on to coach at Columbia University.

Labels on photo: SCHEIB, GAYLORD, MEEKS, ALVIS, MOORE, KEMERER, BULLMAN, McBRIDE, STARDOM, SIMMONS, CARR

BULLMAN BREAKING THRU - Smothere CARRS PASS. Wesleyan-7 Syracuse-3

The 1924 football team lost only two games (to West Virginia University and Waynesburg College), but defeated national contender Syracuse University and Southern Methodist University in the "Dixie Classic," a forerunner to the Cotton Bowl.

Notes

1. Thomas Haught, *West Virginia Wesleyan College 1890-1940* (Buckhannon, WV: West Virginia Wesleyan College Press, 1940), 19–20.

2. Kenneth Plummer, *A History of West Virginia Wesleyan College 1890-1965* (Buckhannon, WV: West Virginia Wesleyan College Press, 1965), 19.

3. Haught, 36–38.

4. William B. Cutright, *A History of Upshur County from its Earliest Exploration and Settlement to the Present Time* (1907), 268.

5. Haught, 44.

6. Haught, 45.

7. Haught, 54.

8. West Virginia Conference Seminary, *First Annual Catalog of the West Virginia Conference Seminary* (Wheeling, WV: Prohibition Press), 36.

9. Ibid., 13.

10. Haught, 63.

11. Kent Kessler, *Hail West Virginians!* (Parkersburg, WV: Park Press, 1959), 129.

12. Plummer, 38.

13. Haught, 70–71.

14. West Virginia Wesleyan College, *Board of Trustee Minutes*, November 15, 1899.

15. Haught, 181–182.

16. Carl Doney, *Cheerful Yesterdays and Confident Tomorrows* (Portland, OR: Binfords & Mort, 1942), 102–105.

17. Thomas Haught, *West Virginia Wesleyan College The Sixth Decade 1940-1950* (Buckhannon, WV: West Virginia Wesleyan College Press: 1950), 13.

18. "Dr. Cutshall's Health Improving," *Pharos* (Buckhannon, WV), September 24, 1924.

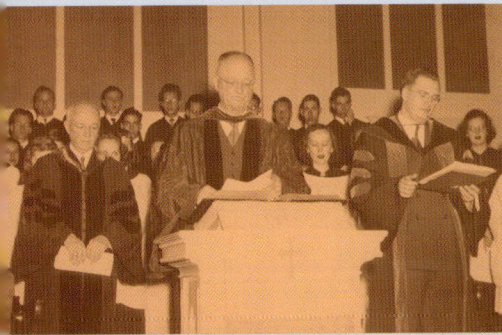

CHAPTER 2

Weathering the Storm

While Wesleyan's earliest years were fraught with financial uncertainty, never was its survival more in doubt than through the tumultuous period of the Great Depression. The trickle-down effect from the October 1929 stock market crash was slower to reach Buckhannon, but the college was already in the precarious position of heavy indebtedness and cumulative deficits for a few years through the end of Homer Wark's presidency. Wark's successor, Roy McCuskey (Sem. 1905; College 1908), served numerous Methodist Episcopal churches throughout West Virginia and had been approached about Wesleyan's presidency in 1926. He reluctantly agreed to run, though neither he nor the other candidate secured enough votes, and Wark was elected as a compromise to break the stalemate. Asked to run again in 1931, he agreed, though not without substantial personal reservations about his experience, his ability as an administrator, and his decision to leave the pastorate. He was nonetheless elected unanimously by the board, which was pleased to have a native West Virginia Methodist clergyman as president for the first time.

1931–1956

McCuskey received assurance of support from the board and was greeted by enthusiastic applause when he entered the Agnes Howard Hall dining room for the first time after his election. That outpouring of goodwill and excitement was quickly tempered by the stark reality of the college's situation. The stock market crash led to the failure of every bank in Upshur County, save one, and the college had difficulty securing credit for its continued operation. The endowment at the time, already small for an institution of Wesleyan's size, was dealt a serious blow. In October of 1931, one month into his presidency, McCuskey was forced to call for faculty and staff of Wesleyan to voluntarily return 5 percent of their salary to the institution. Further incremental salary cuts became necessary in 1932 and 1933, so that within three years every employee's salary had been cut by nearly 45 percent.[1]

The college also regularly struggled to meet payroll; when employees were paid, it was often only in part. Severe conditions in the spring of 1931 led to the layoff of all but two maintenance and grounds workers. Providing even basic services became a struggle, and at one point the local store providing food for the dining room in Agnes Howard Hall refused to accept the college's credit, demanding cash only. Enrollment sagged through the mid-1930s, as students and parents simply could not afford the cost of college. Those students who did attend

Right: Originally from Wheeling, West Virginia, Roy McCuskey was instrumental in leading the college through the Great Depression.

Below: The campus through the 1930s included the old president's home in the foreground (left) grove of trees and "Old Smokey," the campus heating plant, visible behind the Administration Building.

"WESLEYAN" '26

Football retained a heavy focus in the 1920s and 1930s, though that emphasis got the college in trouble with its accreditors by 1932.

often required substantial aid, which the college struggled to provide. Many were forced to leave school prematurely or interrupt their attendance.

In addition to its financial woes, Wesleyan suffered a serious setback when the North Central Association revoked its accreditation in the fall of 1932. Financial insolvency was cited as one contributing factor, though the primary concern involved residual problems regarding athletics. Money raised by athletic alumni was now loaned to student athletes, though poor oversight led many students to incorrectly believe they were being given scholarships they did not need to repay. While a loan board was created to more closely monitor the system, the North Central Association mandated that all loans be discontinued immediately. McCuskey felt it was unfair to completely cut off aid to students already struggling to meet educational expenses, and eventually disregarded the association's edict after appealing unsuccessfully for temporary leniency.

A tennis court was one of the earliest additions to campus, making the sport a popular activity for both men and women, as seen here in 1931.

To boost morale, President McCuskey began observing Arbor Day as early as 1932, planting a new tree annually on the campus grounds.

Despite these enormous hardships, Roy McCuskey characterized the period as one of patient understanding, neighborly concern, and mutual sacrifice.[2] As much as possible, students were given campus jobs to help defray tuition costs. In exchange for yard work or gardening, some administrators and faculty provided housing for male students who could not afford boarding elsewhere. Faculty doubled up on administrative work to save positions, and many of them put their own future educational plans on hold until the economic situation eased. While it would have been easy for despondency to take hold, McCuskey's positive attitude, dogged determination, and devotion to the mission of Wesleyan were critical to maintaining campus morale through the Great Depression.

The "Swinging Bridge," seen behind these two students playing on the ice of the Buckhannon River in 1934, was a popular gathering spot.

The college continued to thrive academically with the addition of well-respected, dynamic faculty members such as Nicholas Hyma in chemistry. Arriving in 1919, he quickly won great affection through his congenial personality and conscientiousness toward student concerns. In an uncommon stance for the time, he encouraged women as equally as men to enter the sciences. So great was his love of teaching and of his field that, when offered a lucrative (at the time) five-figure salary to take a job at a private chemical company, he stated, "I declined the offer because I would rather teach West Virginia boys and girls chemistry."[3] By 1951, Wesleyan was ranked thirty-seventh out of the top fifty colleges and universities in the country for students pursuing graduate education or careers in the sciences.[4] Harold Almond, campus physician, recounted Hyma's final hours before suffering a massive heart attack in 1956: "Whether he knew it or not it is hard to say, but he called me back the second time that night and grasped my hand saying, 'Tell them to carry on (at the College),' and twenty minutes later he had left us."[5] Hyma's love of Wesleyan and of teaching was such that he asked for his ashes to be spread around the foundation of Haymond Hall of Science.

The late 1930s saw Wesleyan begin to turn a long, slow corner toward recovery. Faculty salaries gradually regained some of their tremendous early decade losses, and student enrollment began increasing again in 1936.

A major in business administration was added in 1940, and the department of Christian education and church leadership was established in 1942. Chapel services remained mandatory, though were reduced in frequency from three services per week to one in 1937. Cultural organizations enriched campus life, while their outreach bolstered Wesleyan's reputation across the state. The Wesleyan Playshop, founded in 1928, came to greater prominence after Grace Neil (known to many as Mrs. C. Edmund Neil) became the director in 1933. Students staged many contemporary and sometimes unorthodox dramas, though they were well produced and

James Judson (standing), seen here in a biology laboratory during the 1930s, was one of a number of faculty members who helped Wesleyan emerge as a leader in the sciences.

frequently met with acclaim on campus and in the community. Similarly, under the leadership of noted music educator Marie Boette, a new *a cappella* choir was formed around 1936 to revive that type of singing.

As the 1930s progressed, a development in Methodism led to new, difficult questions about Wesleyan's role and place in the state's educational landscape. The schism of the church during the Civil War over the issue of slavery was resolved with a reunification of the Methodist Episcopal Church, Methodist Protestant Church, and Methodist Episcopal Church, South in 1939 into

Choir members, shown in 1933 at the Methodist Episcopal Church in Fairmont, West Virginia, frequently toured the mid-Atlantic states recruiting for Wesleyan.

Atkinson Chapel doubled as a theatre for Wesleyan's Playshop, which produced *Blind Alley* in 1940, starring future Wesleyan president Ronald Sleeth (1942, seated).

the Methodist Church. The Methodist Episcopal Church, South established Morris Harvey College around the same time as Wesleyan and, as early as 1925, Methodists in both branches began questioning the need for two church-related schools in West Virginia. When Morris Harvey moved from Barboursville to Charleston, West Virginia, in 1935, proponents of a single school, and especially those who sought to boost the capital's economic interests, began more aggressively advocating that Wesleyan and Morris Harvey merge in Charleston.

Right: One-time Wesleyan student Susanne Fisher, flanked by President McCuskey (left) and professor Ralph Brown (right), returned for a campus performance in 1936 after making her Metropolitan Opera debut in Puccini's *Madame Butterfly*.

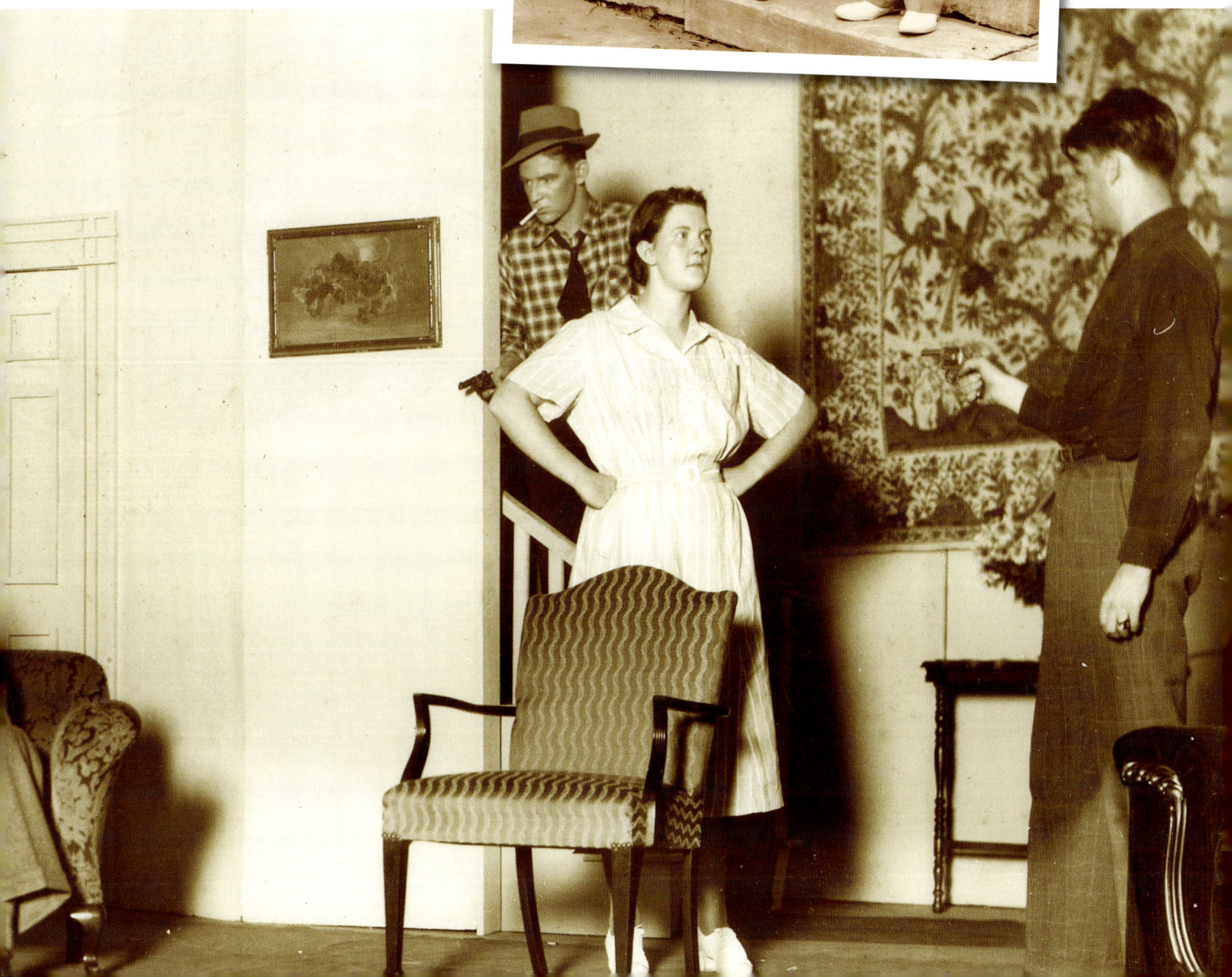

A campus springhouse was removed in 1938 after the spring that fed it dried up.

Cordial conversations between the presidents of both schools led a national Methodist Board of Education Commission in 1941 to recommend a merger in Buckhannon instead.[6] Before the Methodist Annual Conference could approve the commission's recommendation, Morris Harvey College withdrew from the Methodist Church completely and became a privately funded, non-sectarian school, eventually changing its name to the University of Charleston.

Having navigated the reunification of Methodism and the uncertainty surrounding the possible merger, Roy McCuskey began to consider resignation in 1939 after some health problems emerged. The board asked him to remain until the college celebrated its semi-centennial in 1940, which he did. One aspect of the celebration was a $1 million campaign to construct a library, retire indebtedness, and return the endowment to a pre-Depression level. The campaign was spearheaded by former president Wallace B. Fleming,

who returned to Wesleyan in 1937 as vice president specifically for that purpose.

No new buildings were constructed between 1929 and 1947, though McCuskey and Fleming were responsible for cultivating two major gifts that led to expansion nearly a decade later. Around 1939, a surprise bequest of $200,000 appeared from the estate of Calvin A. West of Florida. West spent one year in Buckhannon in his youth and, as a devout Methodist, felt it was important to help young people attend college by providing scholarship support. McCuskey and Fleming met with his widow, Mary Lowe West, later in 1939, and she indicated she wished to fund a memorial chapel on campus in addition to her husband's gift. Though a chapel was not completed until 1967, the college received approximately $100,000 as a provision of West's will in 1948. Fleming and McCuskey also made initial connection with Annie Merner Pfeiffer, visiting her at her home in New York.

Annie Merner Pfeiffer, widow of chemical company owner Henry Pfeiffer and benefactress of Wesleyan's new library, never set foot on Wesleyan's campus.

Pfeiffer was a benefactress of many Methodist institutions, and McCuskey and Fleming saw an opportunity to secure funding for a freestanding library. The current facility was basically unchanged since 1906—an undersized double room on the second floor of the Administration Building which was inadequate for the growing student body and the type of work being done.

When McCuskey resigned the presidency in June 1941, Wallace Fleming was the natural choice to step in as acting president. His second, much shorter, term brought about re-accreditation by the North Central Association in 1942, something McCuskey had worked hard to see accomplished. By April 1942, the board had chosen Joseph Warren Broyles to lead the college as its next president. With Fleming as vice president again, Broyles continued the successful legacy of fundraising and solicitation established by McCuskey.

A third major gift of the period began to solidify with interest from the Loar family of Oakland, Maryland. In 1906, a seventeen-year-old named Ethel Ray Loar enrolled at Wesleyan.

Joseph Warren Broyles, a Methodist clergyman originally from Tennessee, came to Wesleyan from Snead Junior College in Alabama, where he served as president.

The daughter of successful businessman and bank executive Lawson Leolidus Loar and his wife Virginia Lee Wright Loar, Ethel Ray was forced to withdraw from school after only one semester due to rheumatoid arthritis. She spent the rest of her life confined to her parents' home and died in 1930. Though Lawson and Virginia had discussed support of Wesleyan, Lawson's death in 1939 saw no provision for Wesleyan, but rather the stipulation that his substantial estate be used primarily for the upkeep of a neglected cemetery in Grafton, West Virginia. Virginia Loar decided to support the college through donation of some property in Clarksburg and later pledged $100,000 to construct a music building as a memorial to her daughter. After contesting Lawson's will, she placed further funds in trust as an endowment for the L. L. Loar and Family Memorial Music Building.

By 1958, Virginia Lee Loar, along with her children, contributed over $650,000 to Wesleyan in building, scholarship, and endowment support.

WORLD WAR II AND WESLEYAN

In March 1943, Buckhannon welcomed the first 350 trainees of the Forty-ninth Army Air Corps Detachment to West Virginia Wesleyan College. Coming from all over the country, the cadets were a mix of generally college-aged women and men (many combat-ineligible) who were trained in one of three areas: air combat services; as aides to draftsmen, engineers, or chemists; or as cadet nurses in partnership with St. Mary's Hospital in Clarksburg, West Virginia. At the end of a ten-week session, trainees were transferred to Wright Field in Dayton, Ohio, and immediately entered work in airplane design or construction or were deployed as pilots. The college invested in the expansion of the old Lewis airstrip on Brushy Fork Road in order to facilitate the mandatory ten-hour flying time requirement for the air combat students. Cadets were not considered Wesleyan students and were subject to military regulation, including regular room inspections, prescribed sleeping and eating periods, and regular drill on the athletic fields. By the time the program had concluded in 1945, Wesleyan had played host to 1,339 cadets.

(Photos courtesy of the Upshur County Historical Society)

The December 7, 1941, bombing of Pearl Harbor, Hawaii, and America's subsequent entrance into the Second World War put many of the college's plans on hold. It did not take long for the campus to be swept up in the national movement of frenzied patriotism. Student organizations bought war bonds and updates appeared in the *Pharos* about enlisted classmates. As male student enrollment plummeted due to enlistment and conscription, the college was kept afloat when the government assigned the Forty-ninth College Training Detachment (Aircrew) to Wesleyan beginning in March 1943. For two years Wesleyan hosted a mix of traditional students and cadets from elsewhere in the country training for various engineering, drafting, chemist, and nursing support roles in the Army Air Corps at Wright Field in Dayton, Ohio.

Unlike the First World War, when the gymnasium was converted into a barracks, Wesleyan's female student population was displaced from Agnes Howard Hall to various Buckhannon residences and recently vacated fraternity houses. Despite strict regulations for the cadets, Wesleyan students had occasional opportunities to mingle with the campus guests at chaperoned dances and other social events.

By the war's end in September 1945, Wesleyan lost not only twenty-six of its students and alumni to the conflict, but its president as well. Joseph Warren Broyles died on September 29, 1945, after suffering a heart attack at his Buckhannon home. Bishop James Straughn memorialized Broyles at an October 18, 1945, service for Wesleyan's fallen students that Broyles himself had helped to plan. He was remembered as a stabilizing influence

With most all of the fraternity brothers away at war, the Kappa Alpha house at 49 South Florida Street, seen here in 1938, temporarily became a women's residence hall in 1943.

during a period of great upheaval, and his short tenure was punctuated by the news of Annie Merner Pfeiffer's gift of $100,000 (later $150,000) in 1944 toward a new library. Her gift was contingent on two other buildings of equal cost being constructed prior to receiving the money. Pfeiffer died just months after Broyles in January 1946, and her estate was executed by the Board of Education of the Methodist Church, which eventually allowed Wesleyan to construct the other two buildings in close succession, rather than simultaneously.

In anticipation of the large numbers of returning soldiers who would be taking advantage of government incentives to receive a college education on the G.I. Bill, Wesleyan found itself in desperate need of temporary housing. With assistance from the Federal Housing Authority, thirteen housing units were constructed in 1946. Five units were built near Haymond Hall of Science to house seventy-four single men and another eight units, consisting of thirty-two apartments for married students, were built on the present site of the Benedum and Holloway Residence Halls. These units remained until the end of the 1957–1958 school year.

In 1947, a government surplus army barracks from Point Pleasant, West Virginia, was shipped to campus and reassembled near the current site of the L. L. Loar and Family Memorial Music Building. Its purpose was to become Wesleyan's first official student union, an idea that originated from the establishment of a PX (post exchange) for the visiting cadets in one of the violin studios of the Annex Building. When the air corps left, Wesleyan students asked if the former mess hall in the basement of the gymnasium could be converted into a recreation room. An adjoining small swimming pool, which the fire marshal had recently condemned, was shortly thereafter converted into a smoking room. The inadequacy of the gymnasium and a growing movement among students for a permanent gathering space led the college to acquire the modest, yet functional barracks building. It contained a snack bar/soda fountain, recreation room, dance floor, bookstore, health center, and offices for student publications.

Wesleyan, like the rest of the nation, struggled with the issue of race relations through the late 1940s and 1950s. Progressive members of the faculty thought Wesleyan should move to accept African-American students, though they were unsure of the climate among members of the board and anticipated resistance. Believing a small change was better than no change

DOROTHY LEE SCHOLARSHIP FOR OVERSEAS STUDENTS

The Dorothy Lee Scholarship for Overseas Students had humble beginnings as a group of college administrators and alumni attempting to raise funds to enroll the daughter of Dorothy Lee (1927, below right), Wesleyan's first Chinese graduate. Lee returned to China after marrying Dr. James Cheng, who served at one time as attending physician to Chiang Kai-shek. In the wake of the Japanese invasion of China in 1937 and the later outbreak of World War II, the family was desperate to get their daughter out of the country. By 1946, a committee (which included Wallace B. Fleming and Roy McCuskey) secured funding for Julia B. Cheng (below left) to enroll and she graduated in the class of 1950. Further support from Edna Jenkins (Sem. 1902) and many others allowed the program to expand its reach to other international students. Starting in 1990, flags from the home countries of Wesleyan's international students have been displayed in the gymnasium.

With the married student barracks in the background, members of the trustees broke ground on the L. L. Loar and Family Memorial Music Building in 1950.

A 1952 competition to name the student center ended with the acronym S.C.O.W. (Student Center of Wesleyan), much to the chagrin of administration, which felt the association with a garbage boat was unbecoming.

at all, they brought a motion to the trustees asking that qualified *local* African-American students *living in their homes* be allowed to enroll at Wesleyan. With only minor dissention, the board bypassed the faculty's concerns and voted to completely integrate in March 1949. This made Wesleyan the first non-historically black college or university in the state to integrate, a full five years prior to the landmark *Brown vs. Board of Education* ruling.[7] A small number of unsympathetic board members, in an attempt to derail the effort, indicated that no such resolution to integrate was necessary since there was no explicit statement in any college policy forbidding African-American students from attending. This reasoning was rejected and the first four African-American students enrolled in the fall of 1949.

Though Buckhannon historically had a larger population of African Americans, only a small enclave remained by 1949. The segregated Victoria School closed that year due to low student enrollment, and African-American students either traveled to Clarksburg to attend school or lived with relatives in other towns. Despite general support for integration, there remained some tension among campus and community members; a few board members even resigned over the issue. The administration complicated the situation in the years that followed by not immediately allowing African-American students to take advantage of campus housing and dining facilities. After pressure from student organizations, fraternities, sororities, Community Council, and the dean, the board reaffirmed its earlier decision to integrate and instructed the administration to open all college accommodations equally to African-American students in 1954.[8]

After the death of President Broyles in 1945, Dean Arthur Allen Schoolcraft temporarily filled the presidency until the board elected William John Scarborough in August 1946. Meeting the "two building" requirement of the Annie Merner Pfeiffer bequest became the top priority of his administration. A movement was

Bishop James Straughn (left) and former president Wallace B. Fleming (center) joined in the November 1946 inauguration of William Scarborough (right).

The local Masonic Lodge laid the cornerstone of the Annie Merner Pfeiffer Library in 1950.

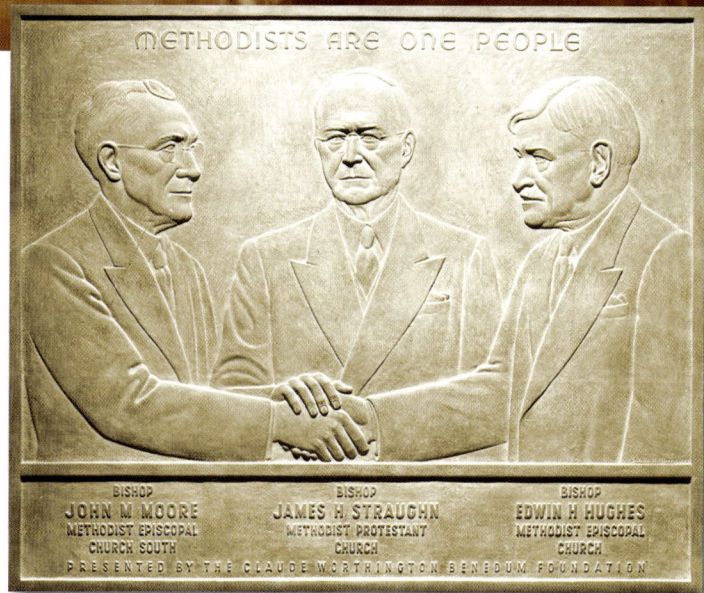

A bronze plaque by Julian Hoke Harris commemorating the 1939 Methodist reunification was dedicated in 1953 and installed in the first floor of the Annie Merner Pfeiffer Library.

already afoot at the end of Broyles's presidency to raise $200,000 for a men's dormitory. With that money in hand by 1947, the first new construction on campus since 1929 began on what would become Fleming Hall. The building started an unofficial tradition during the period of naming new men's residence halls after former presidents of Wesleyan. As the Loar gift materialized, the new music building became the second structure to satisfy the Pfeiffer bequest. In order to have cash in hand to construct the music building and library, the trustees authorized an emergency fundraising campaign. This effort was aided by the Methodist Church, which saw an opportunity to move their conference sessions to Wesleyan, provided the college could complete the necessary campus additions. Fleming Hall was available for occupancy in the fall of 1952 and the L. L. Loar and Family Memorial Music Building was

dedicated in March 1953. The Methodist Annual Conference arrived on Wesleyan's campus in May 1953 and dedicated the Annie Merner Pfeiffer Library on their first day of meetings.

The outbreak of the Korean War in 1950 stalled some of Wesleyan's positive momentum. The large wave of new students immediately after the Second World War quickly diminished as young men found themselves headed overseas yet again. Unlike the previous two world wars, no army training program existed to offset the loss of male students who were deployed. The 1951 football season was cancelled entirely, and the total enrollment fell to a dangerously low 397 students by the fall of 1952, down from a peak of nearly eight hundred in 1948. The death of Cecil B. "Cebe" Ross (1923) in 1953 was another blow to campus. Ross was an all-around student athlete at Wesleyan before returning in 1925 as the coach of all sports and later athletic director. While the West Virginia Intercollegiate Athletic Conference (WVIAC) was formed in 1924 just prior to Ross's return, he helped facilitate the move of the WVIAC basketball tournament to Wesleyan in 1939. To honor Ross's accomplishments on the field and as a coach, the board of trustees passed a resolution in March 1957 naming the football field in his memory.

The remainder of President Scarborough's term was spent helping Wesleyan recover from its difficulties during the Korean War and planning for future development. Enrollment losses, coupled with a lower national birthrate trend and changes to the G.I. Bill for Korean War veterans, meant Wesleyan had to be proactive in its search for new students. President Scarborough and Dean Schoolcraft organized "Goodwill Caravans" of students who traveled to nearly three hundred Methodist churches and Sunday schools throughout West Virginia and western Pennsylvania to recruit for Wesleyan. The program yielded steady growth through the mid-1950s, bringing enrollment back to post-World War II levels.

Left: The marching band, seen here in 1954, frequently participated in the Homecoming parade, an annual tradition that originated around 1928 and continued into the early 2000s.

Below: The tradition of a singing competition during the May Day festival started in 1949. Seen here are the 1955 May Sing champions in the independent women's division.

Scarborough also realized the necessity of strategic planning in the wake of the recent building construction and he established a commission to vision the college's future to its seventy-fifth anniversary in 1965. The commission's work, in the short term, led to the purchase of the old tannery site to create athletic practice fields in 1954. The planning team also established a trajectory of growth, identifying the need for a new gymnasium, a new science building, a chapel, and more residence halls. After a decade of service, Scarborough resigned the presidency in 1956, having successfully set the stage for an unparalleled period of development for the college.

Top: The Wesleyan basketball team in 1938, which was also the last year the state high school basketball tournament was held at Wesleyan. The WVIAC basketball tournament moved to Buckhannon the following year and remained until 1960.

Right: Dinner was always a semi-formal occasion, as evidenced by these students gathered in the basement dining room of Agnes Howard Hall around Thanksgiving in 1956.

Below: As the dean and registrar, Arthur Allen Schoolcraft individually advised most students and was responsible for the addition of a bachelor of music education degree in 1951 and a library science major in 1950.

Notes

1. Roy McCuskey, *All Things Work Together for Good to Those That Love God* (Buckhannon, WV: West Virginia Wesleyan College Press, 1964), 103.

2. McCuskey, 104–105.

3. H. Eugene Modlin and Mary Sumner Modlin, "Wesleyan in the 1920s," *Sundial*, March 1966, 22.

4. Goodrich, Knapp, and Boehm, "The Origin of U.S. Scientists," *Scientific American*, July 1951, 16.

5. West Virginia Wesleyan College Office of Alumni Affairs, *Nicholas Hyma Professor of Chemistry 1919-1956.* (Buckhannon, WV: West Virginia Wesleyan College, November 1956), 9.

6. McCuskey, 119–120.

7. James M. Trimmer, "W. Va. College to End Segregation," *Christian Century*, May 25, 1949, 659.

8. Arthur Allen Schoolcraft, "A Statement and a Plea by the Dean of the College to the Board of Trustees," a report issued to the trustees dated March 12, 1954, 6–7.

CHAPTER 3

An Era of Growth

Despite adverse conditions through its first sixty-seven years, Wesleyan made noteworthy progress on a number of fronts. Academic offerings diversified, the physical plant expanded, new co-curricular and athletic activities enriched campus life, and the connection with the Methodist Church yielded not only financial support, but also students and leadership at all levels of the college. There was a sense of anxious optimism by early 1957 as the board deliberated on who would lead the campus next. Few could have anticipated the massive explosion of growth and development in all areas that would accompany the tenure of Wesleyan's longest-serving president.

A watercolor by art professor Fred Messersmith (right) was presented to college benefactress Edna Jenkins (Sem. 1902) at the dedication of Jenkins Hall, named in her honor in 1959.

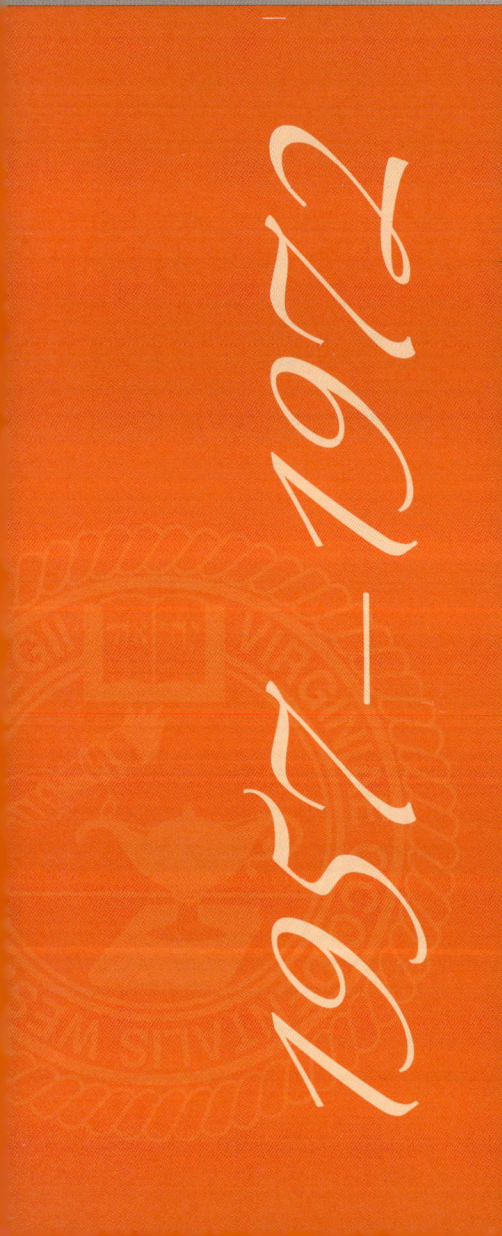

1957–1972

In February 1957, the board of trustees selected Stanley Hubert Martin as the eleventh president of the college. In addition to being a Methodist clergyman, Martin brought seven years of experience from the Methodist Board of Education as the executive secretary of the Department of Student Loans, Scholarships, and Personnel. Along with his wife Glenadine and their two children, Martin relocated to Buckhannon in March 1957 and set to work on the task of long-range planning that would become a hallmark of his presidency. Though Martin was committed to growing the enrollment, he felt Wesleyan's small size and close-knit community atmosphere were qualities to be valued and preserved. As an advocate for true, comprehensive liberal arts education, Martin felt Wesleyan's curriculum had lost some of its focus and effectiveness. Rather than a strategic vision for student learning, he saw a curriculum that favored the addition of too many new and sometimes arbitrary courses to suit faculty research and teaching interests. Martin was also adamant the college should retain its historic ties to the Methodist Church and the church, in turn, should embrace Wesleyan as its college in West Virginia by supporting it with students and its finances.

The college outsourced its food service to SAGA in 1958 after building two kitchen/dining room facilities, one in McCuskey Hall and one in Jenkins Hall, seen here in 1964.

The trustees had already committed to making Wesleyan more residential, bringing male students on-campus with the construction of Fleming Hall in 1952. By the time the board agreed to construct another men's residence hall in 1956, the college was able to take advantage of a new source of federal loan funding offered through the Housing and Home Finance Agency. The availability of this capital made it possible to build McCuskey Hall, which opened in 1958, followed by a number of new dormitories and other buildings in relatively quick succession. A contract was awarded in the summer of 1957 for construction of a new residence hall for women, which was named Jenkins Hall at its dedication in 1959.

In addition to administrative roles, Stanley Martin previously served as a religious education professor at Boston University and as a campus minister at the Wesley Foundation at the University of Iowa.

In some ways Stanley Martin was a staunch traditionalist. He placed great emphasis on the concept of the "Wesleyan Family" and sought to preserve standards of community living that he felt developed and strengthened the character of students. Even after the addition of new dining rooms in Jenkins and McCuskey Halls, great strains were placed on the campus dining service. Stanley Martin fought hard to maintain Wesleyan's tradition of served meals, only reluctantly allowing the move to cafeteria-style as the growing student body made any other arrangement impossible. A student dress code also mandated specific attire for different occasions and times of day. Dinner required more formal dress, while concerts, socials, and church were more formal still. It wasn't until 1968 for men and 1969 for women that many of these restrictions were rolled back by the Community Council.

LARSON AND LARSON ARCHITECTS

Hired to be the campus architects in 1958, the Winston-Salem, North Carolina, firm of Larson and Larson was largely responsible for the predominant Neo-Georgian architectural style of the campus. Red brick, white columns, prominent but understated pediments, and the use of cupolas are unifying hallmarks of the campus visual identity. Larson and Larson was also responsible for developing the first campus master plan, which became instrumental in guiding future physical expansion.

Faculty housing, seen here in an architectural rendering, was one of many additions to the campus which never came to fruition. Other such projects included separate education and home economics buildings, married student housing, a riverside amphitheater, a nine-hole golf course, a president's home at the end of the mall, a boathouse, and an equestrian center.

In 1962, at the cost of $8,000, Larson and Larson constructed a four-foot by four-foot scale model projecting future campus development. The model was displayed under a plastic bubble for many years in the Lynch-Raine Administration Building.

The choir, under director Irma Helen Hopkins in 1964, was a feature of weekly chapel services in Atkinson Auditorium.

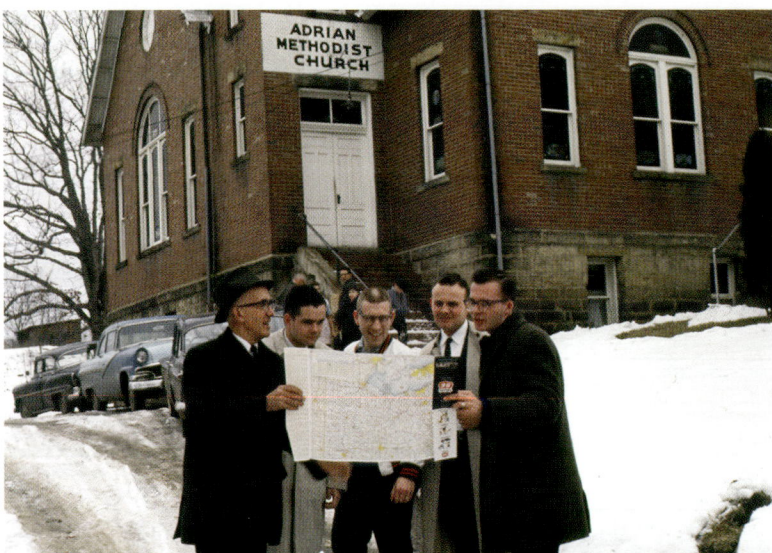

At its peak, the Town and Country program placed pre-ministerial students and Christian educators in nearly 150 local churches. Ralph Grieser (left), seen here in 1964, was named the program's director in 1961.

Weekly chapel service was still considered foundational to student development, though the growing student body made logistics difficult. As early as 1962, the administration was compelled to provide separate chapel gatherings for Catholic students (with the priest from Holy Rosary Catholic Church) and Jewish students (with religion professor Ralph Brown), while Protestant students met in Atkinson Chapel. Student involvement in religious life was high, and an umbrella group called Religious Life Council (RLC) was formed during the 1959–1960 school year. RLC paralleled the function of Community Council and brought together the Christian Greek letter organizations Kappa Phi and Sigma Theta Epsilon, the chaplains of the social Greek letter organizations, other organizations

such as Methodist Student Movement, and faculty representatives to plan religious programming, such as Religious Emphasis Week, and to discuss issues of religious and social concern.

Throughout Stanley Martin's administration, enrollment growth created a cyclical pattern of campus development that lead to further enrollment growth. As the campus population passed the one-thousand-student mark for the first time in 1959–1960 and prospects remained high for continued expansion, a rear addition to Fleming Hall was constructed in 1960, along with a new dormitory, Doney Hall, to create an open quad of residence halls. Another women's dormitory was completed in 1963, carrying the moniker "New Hall" for nearly three years until it was officially named Holloway Hall by the trustees in 1966. Fred Holloway was the first bishop of the West Virginia Annual Conference after it had been administratively separated from the Pittsburgh Area and made into its own conference in 1960. As with all future West Virginia and Pittsburgh Area bishops, Holloway served as an ex-officio member of Wesleyan's board.

President Martin (left) looked on as Bishop Fred Holloway (center) and Board Chair Myron Hymes (right) helped place the cornerstone of Doney Hall at an October 1961 ceremony.

Founded in 1961, the Emeritus Club is open to Wesleyan graduates of fifty years or more. Seen here in 1966, members continue to meet regularly and support college programs and facilities.

The name S.C.O.W. was transferred from the old barracks to the third-floor coffee shop of the new student center, seen here in 1963, which contained a jukebox and access to a roof deck.

The student-led Campus Center Programming Board, along with a staff director, managed logistics of the campus center, including the six-lane bowling alley located on the first floor.

Martin was hopeful that new residence halls would allow the college to raze the 1890 College Avenue wing of Agnes Howard Hall and renovate the 1929 Meade Street addition. By 1960, he expressed a similar desire to see the aging Annex Building demolished because of its architectural incongruity with the rest of campus, and it was intentionally left out of the campus master plan. Yet both buildings survived as other developments took precedence. A better student union was one such priority. Though the temporary barracks that housed the S.C.O.W. was a veritable hive of activity at any time of day, it became increasingly difficult to hold events there as the student body grew. With close to $445,000 of total funding from the Claude Worthington Benedum Foundation, groundbreaking on the Benedum Campus Community Center was held in the spring of 1961. The design included an impressive number of amenities: a game room, music listening rooms, a reading room with current newspapers and magazines, a junior Olympic-sized swimming pool, a large social hall, and the campus radio station, bookstore, and post office. Student morale soared when the building was opened in 1963.

Football, basketball, and baseball—sports historically at the core of Wesleyan's athletic program—were joined by a growing list of new offerings. A men's swimming team formed in 1964 after the new campus center swimming pool opened, and Wesleyan became a powerhouse, winning state championships in 1967, 1968, and 1969. The men's tennis team captured WVIAC

Above: The football team of 1961 was the only one in a period of sixty years (1935–1995) to win a WVIAC championship.

Left: A women's field hockey team, started in 1963–1964, was the only intercollegiate sport for women until a swimming team was added in 1972–1973.

championships in 1962 and 1964 after new tennis courts were added behind Fleming and Haymond Halls in 1961. A brand new men's soccer team made history on October 30, 1959, playing the first intercollegiate soccer game in West Virginia and losing to Fairmont State College. Fairmont State's team had played previously, but their matches had all been out-of-state.[1] By 1965, men's soccer was recognized officially as a WVIAC sport, and Wesleyan promptly won back-to-back championships in

1965 and 1966. Though the number of women involved in intramural sports rivaled that of men, a clear gender gap in intercollegiate sports, in existence since the school's founding, persisted well into the 1980s.

Progress on campus wasn't just limited to new buildings and sports. In early 1961, Stanley Martin directed Miss George Rast to work in conjunction with the former Union Protestant Hospital in Clarksburg, West Virginia, to develop a nursing program for

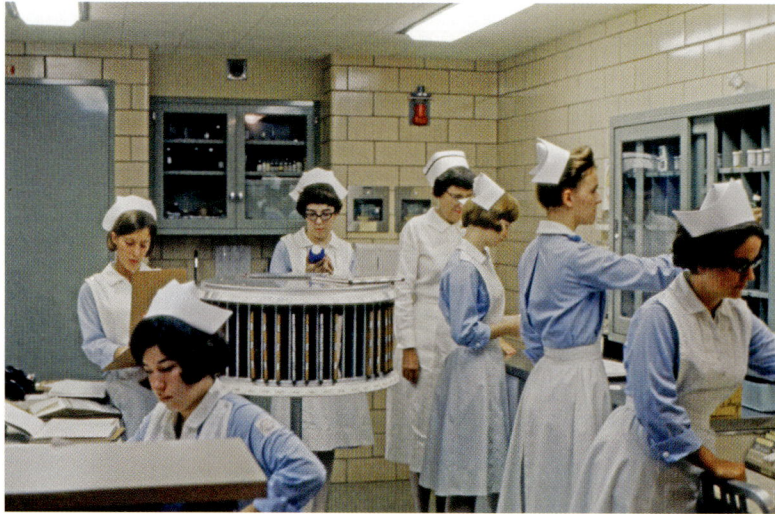

Regular clinical rotations, such as this one at Union Protestant Hospital in Clarksburg, West Virginia, in 1966, were included in the nursing curriculum from the program's beginning.

The first class of five graduated in 1965 and the National League of Nurses accredited the program in 1972.

Stanley Martin and Orlo Strunk Jr. (1953), who replaced Arthur Allen Schoolcraft as dean after Schoolcraft's death in 1959, took many other steps to strengthen the overall academic quality of the school. The registrar function, long a part of the dean's office, was split into a separate position and was filled by Patton Nickell Jr. (1956). As student numbers grew, new faculty members were hired with regularity, while existing faculty saw their salaries improved. The administration highly encouraged professional and academic development among the faculty, providing support for conference attendance, publications,

Wesleyan to begin that fall. Since no facility existed to house the fledgling department, the former Benson residence on Meade Street was purchased in December 1961 (currently the Erickson Alumni Center) for its use. By 1963, a cooperative agreement allowed clinical work in Clarksburg with supervision of faculty members.

Members of the biology honorary Beta Beta Beta pose with their advisor, professor George Rossbach, in the Hudkins-Kelly-Young Museum of Natural Science in 1962. The museum was established in Haymond Hall of Science in 1949.

Prominent anthropologist Margaret Mead (seated) gave a lecture in 1962 and was one of a number of prominent speakers to visit campus through Stanley Martin's presidency.

research, and international travel. A new Learning Center program, founded in 1963 by Phyllis Kohl Coston (1953; Hon. 1998), provided support to any students looking to improve their reading or learning skills.

Upon his arrival at Wesleyan and in many subsequent instances, President Martin posed the hypothetical question, "What type of institution do we want to be?"[2] Answering himself in part, Martin issued his "Expanding Purpose" report in 1964, proposing the most substantial, school-wide curricular revision in the college's history. Citing the lack of any major curriculum update in over twenty-five years and inconsistent course enrollment ranging anywhere from four to ninety-two students in a class, Martin called for the restructuring of departments into eight schools: Religion and Humanities, Business Administration, Education, Music and Art, Physical Education, Social Science, Nursing, and Science.[3]

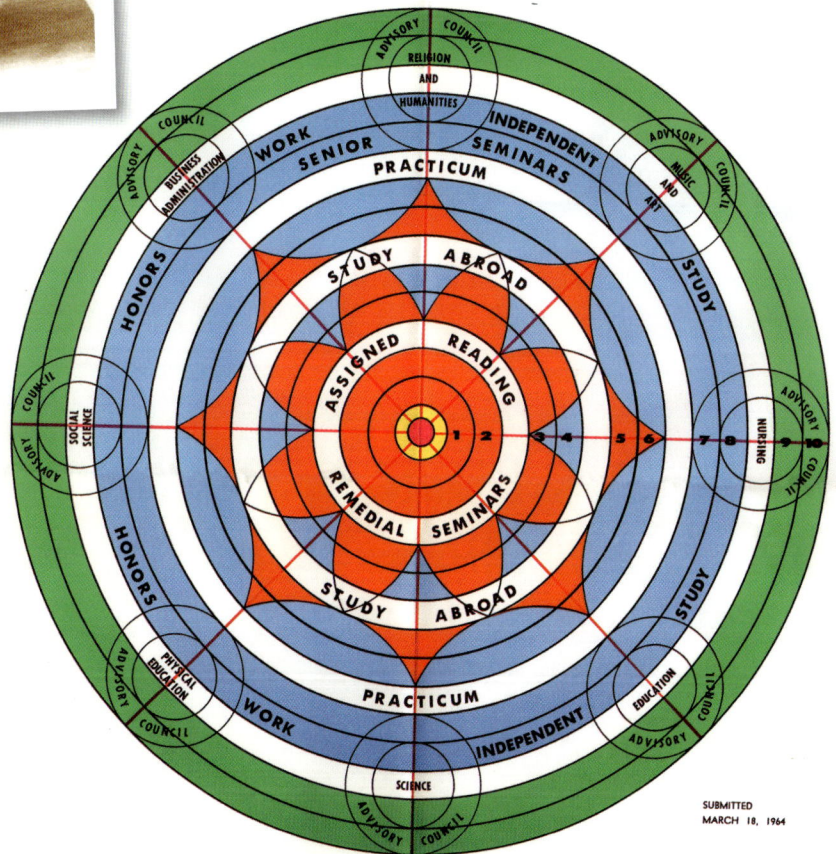

DIAGRAM OF "AN EXPANDING PURPOSE"

A PROPOSED OUTLINE FOR CURRICULAR REVISION SUBMITTED FOR TRUSTEE AND FACULTY CONSIDERATION

WEST VIRGINIA WESLEYAN COLLEGE
BUCKHANNON, WEST VIRGINIA
COLOR DESIGNATIONS OF THE DIAGRAM

| | RELIGION | | LIBERAL STUDIES | | PROFESSIONAL STUDIES |
| | LIBRARY | | SUMMERS | | FIFTH YEAR |

NUMERALS INDICATE SEMESTER SEQUENCE

Stanley Martin's bold "Expanding Purpose" curricular revision of 1964 tried to strike a balance between the liberal arts and the college's expansion into pre-professional programs.

The college's first computer was a 1951 Burroughs model 205 received in 1964. It filled an entire room in a renovated garage that currently houses the Black Student Union and was mostly used for administrative purposes.

required international travel experience. The third and fourth years were to be spent primarily focusing on courses within an academic major with occasional liberal arts courses scattered throughout. The summer between the third and fourth year was to be spent in an internship or directed study placement. Students could graduate after two years of study

The model placed religion and the library as the center of two concentric circles, with a course of study radiating out from there. The first two years were to be spent establishing a liberal arts foundation based on Christian ideals, with a small number of courses in a student's major. The summer between the second and third year was reserved for what was to be a

with an associate of arts degree and students with a B average or higher at the end of four years could extend their study to a fifth year and earn a master of arts degree.

The proposal was implemented slowly, and some elements were not implemented at all. The associate and graduate degree programs were not implemented until the mid-1970s.

ANNIE MERNER PFEIFFER LIBRARY

WESLEYAN ◆ JUBILEE
75 YEARS OF PROGRESS

The Diamond Jubilee Campaign was initiated leading into the college's seventy-fifth birthday in 1965 to raise nearly $1.5 million toward new facilities, including a chapel and science building.

A branch campus in Oxford, England, was explored to support the second/third year foreign travel component, and two faculty members, Duncan Williams and Herbert Coston, went as far as to present possible properties in 1965, though the board took no action. Younger faculty members were added with regularity and, in the spirit of the times, energetically organized to take more direct responsibility for faculty governance, academic policies, curriculum development, and matters of faculty rank and tenure.

The building program continued at a frenzied pace as the long-deferred dream of a dedicated chapel came to fruition. The struggle to secure funding for the $1.1 million facility had been long and difficult, to the extent that, when the board of trustees voted to award the contract in 1965, "President Stanley Martin exclaimed a vociferous 'Amen,' indicating his great joy over the action just taken."[4] The administration felt the chapel should be the physical and intellectual center of the college and, consequently, it straddles the axis between the older front of the campus and the newer section facing Camden Avenue.

The chapel cornerstone was laid in October 1966, and a special dedication service was held in March 1967. The building was named Wesley Chapel because of the Methodist Church's efforts in raising $700,000 toward the facility, though to honor the earlier memorial bequest of Mary Lowe West, a small chapel located on the northeast corner of the building was named the Calvin A. and Mary Lowe West Meditation Chapel. One unique addition to the Meditation Chapel proved to be a major surprise. With the intention of having international and ecumenical symbolism displayed throughout the building, Stanley Martin wrote to a number of agencies and governments soliciting small items representative of various religious traditions around the world that could be displayed. King Hussein of Jordan

Police rescued the brothers of Phi Sigma Epsilon from their East Main Street house after a March 1967 flood inundated much of Buckhannon.

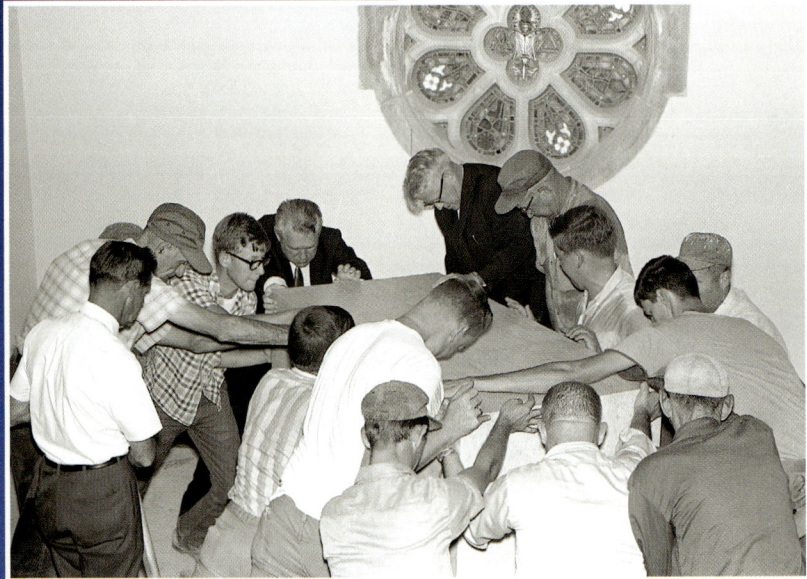

The floor of the West Meditation Chapel had to be reinforced and a crew of fifteen men was required to move the three-ton pink marble altar given to the college by King Hussein of Jordan in 1967.

sent a pink marble stone quarried in the area near Bethlehem, though what arrived was hardly a "stone" in the sense that Stanley Martin imagined. Instead, a three-ton pink marble slab and two other smaller blocks were delivered and became an altar for the Meditation Chapel.

The completion of Wesley Chapel was timely in the larger context of Methodism, as the Methodist Church merged with the Evangelical United Brethren Church in April 1968 to create the United Methodist Church. As the new denomination began the work of integrating buildings, church leadership, and a diverse membership, Wesleyan was chosen to host the first quadrennial Northeastern Jurisdictional Conference where,

Rising above the old S.C.O.W. barracks building, the steeple of Wesley Chapel became the tallest building in Upshur County at 204 feet when it was put into place in 1966.

Wesley Chapel

Wesley Chapel was the centerpiece of Stanley Martin's vision for campus. It seats 1,800 people and is the largest worship space in the state. Stained-glass windows from Blenko Glass of Milton, West Virginia, are one of a number of details that enhance the beauty of the space.

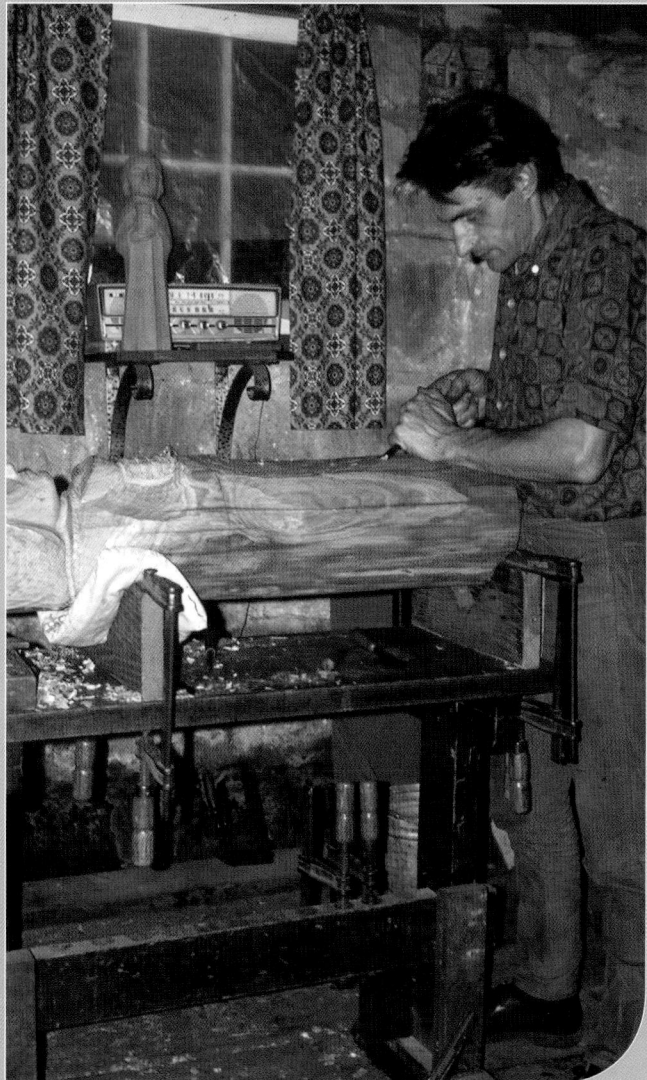

Top left: The original seminary bell was relocated from the Administration Building to the tower of Wesley Chapel. Seen here is President Stanley Martin with Fannie Lynch (Sem. 1901), oldest living alumna of Wesleyan in 1966.

Top right: The eight-foot-tall bronze likeness of John Wesley, displayed as Oxford don rather than in clerical robes, was cast by Julian Hoke Harris and installed in 1967.

Bottom left: A gift of G. I. Rohrbough (1923) in memory of his mother, Etta Maude Lynch Rohrbough (Sem. 1892), the Casavant Freres Ltd. instrument is the largest true pipe organ in the state of West Virginia at 4,244 pipes. Music professor Robert Shafer is seen here preparing for its installation in 1967.

Right: Wolfgang Flor was commissioned to carve the twelve apostles for Wesley Chapel, each represented visually by a unique identifying symbol. Flor used salvaged chestnut logs and stained the figures with acidic mine drainage water to achieve the darker color he desired.

among other things, new bishops are elected. The campus opened its doors to 444 delegates from eleven northeast states and Puerto Rico during the summer of 1968. Two new bishops elected were D. Frederick Wertz and Roy Calvin Nichols, both of whom came to be associated closely with Wesleyan in the years that followed. Wertz was assigned to the West Virginia Annual Conference, while Nichols, the first African-American bishop elected in the new United Methodist Church, was assigned to the Western Pennsylvania Conference. As such, both served as ex-officio members on Wesleyan's board of trustees for twelve years until 1980.

Concurrent with the chapel construction, another women's residence hall was built on Meade Street between L. L. Loar and Family Memorial Music Building and Holloway Hall and was ready for occupancy by the fall of 1967. Like Holloway Hall before, it was known as "New Hall" until it was officially named Paul Gregory Benedum Hall in 1973 to honor the

long-time trustee and benefactor. A pressing facility need was Haymond Hall of Science, which was no longer sufficient for the expanded science programs. A lead gift from Mabel Neville Christopher (1918) and her husband Frank Christopher in memory of their son, H. Ward Christopher, who was killed in a 1962 automobile accident, led to the groundbreaking of Christopher Hall of Science in March 1967.

Even though most of the college's substantial development through the 1960s was set against the backdrop of America's increasing involvement in the war in Vietnam, it was not until the late 1960s that student opinion about the conflict, both around the country and at Wesleyan, began to turn decidedly negative and increasingly vocal. Public support was already declining when the North Vietnamese launched the Tet Offensive in early 1968 and caught American and South Vietnamese troops by surprise. With American casualties mounting and military leaders requesting significant troop

Aging laboratories in Haymond Hall of Science, such as this one in 1963, prompted the college to construct a new science building starting in 1967.

increases, confidence that the stalemated conflict could be quickly resolved eroded even further. Wesleyan students held a silent protest vigil in April 1969. Participants stood on the chapel steps wearing black armbands from 9:00 am until 4:00 pm and Western Pennsylvania Bishop Roy Nichols, who happened to be the chapel speaker for the day, joined the vigil for a short time.

By the fall, anti-war protests grew louder, but also began eliciting some resistance from other segments of the student body. Joining in a national moratorium to end the war on October 15, 1969, Community Council called for a day of anti-war forums, discussions, vigils, and worship services. On the previous day, a number of students asked to hold a funeral procession ending with the burial of a symbolic coffin. The administration allowed the protest and even permitted physical plant workers to dig the hole, yet a group of counter-protesters filled in the hole the night before. Some other students verbally derided the procession as it wound through campus. Undeterred, the protesters re-dug the hole by hand and completed their demonstration.[5] In light of the spring 1970 shooting on the campus of Kent State University, President Martin expressed relief for the

Stanley Martin assembled an informal group of senior faculty in 1964 known as the "Greybeards" to advise him on issues related to the college. Shown here in 1966 are (left to right): William Hallam, George Glauner, Stanley Martin, David E. Reemsnyder, and Arthur Gould.

fact that protests at Wesleyan remained generally civil, focusing more on discourse and mutual understanding rather than inciting vitriol.[6]

The arrival of two dynamic new faculty members, David A. Milburn and Larry R. Parsons in 1966 and 1968 respectively, led the music department in exciting directions. Milburn quickly discovered and fostered student interest in starting a jazz band. While one attempt in 1967 failed, the band finally got off the ground in the spring of 1970 with a five-day tour of the

eastern United States. Parsons, likewise, seized on the existing momentum of Wesleyan's strong choral program, recording an album in his first year and taking the choir, along with Milburn's new brass ensemble, on a European tour in 1970. Many future tours by these and other ensembles became excellent vehicles for recruiting students to Wesleyan's already strong music program.

A new intermester attempted between the fall and spring terms of 1969–1970 served

one of Stanley Martin's earlier goals of expanding international travel opportunities. Trips to South America, the Middle East, and India in January 1970 eventually led to the development of a more comprehensive January Term, or Jan-Term. In addition to international trips, Jan-Term allowed faculty to develop on-campus courses that aligned with their interests and which they might not otherwise have an opportunity to teach; notable examples included Ernest Capstack's course on "Death and Dying," Elizabeth Weimer's course

The tour choir and brass ensemble embarked on an ambitious six-week European tour in the summer of 1970.

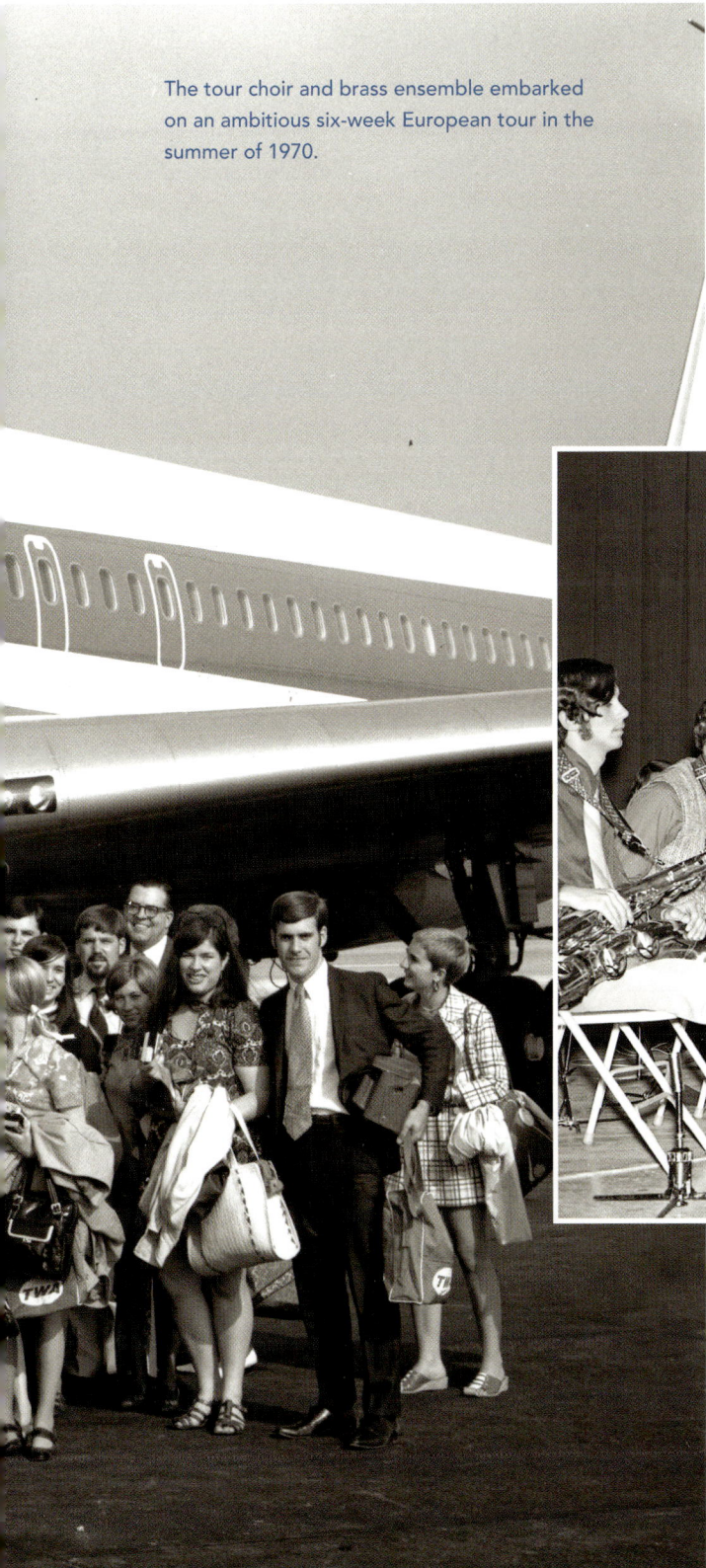

on "Bird Watching," and John Warner's course on "Prison, Courts, and Jails." Theatre and opera productions could be staged because of the scheduling flexibility, and many students completed clinical experiences or contract courses. Jan-Term was a popular option, both because it was included in a student's tuition and also because the schedule format created large blocks of leisure time.

The late 1960s saw major changes in student life. In an ironic twist, the move of chapel services from Atkinson Auditorium into Wesley Chapel made the previous model of mandatory attendance untenable. Despite various attempts to check attendance, the chapel's open pews and student pressure against the requirement made its elimination all but inevitable. Voluntary services were moved to Sunday mornings, and the new Liberal Education Series (L.E.S.), touted by some as chapel's academic and cultural replacement, became one focal point for structured campus gathering. The series brought lecturers, artists,

The jazz band, performing here in 1971, took its first international tour in 1973 and toured Europe on nine other occasions, including performances inside the Soviet bloc during the Cold War.

Arriving on campus as a dorm mother in 1943, Nellie Wilson (Hon. 1983) served as a Christian education professor and dean of women during her thirty-year career. The Associated Women Students asked that the lounge in the Paul G. Benedum Residence Hall be named in her honor in 1969.

musicians, and other academic figures to campus, though attempts to mandate it for all students also eroded through the early 1970s. While not part of the L.E.S., Alex Haley, the co-author of Malcolm X's autobiography and future author of *Roots: The Saga of an American Family*, spoke in 1971.

Stanley Martin's comprehensive vision for campus was only partially realized by 1967. To provide for some of the most pressing needs of the campus master plan, the board approved a nearly $2 million campaign to raise money for a new physical education complex, a new building to house the nursing department, and a humanities/communication addition to the Annie Merner Pfeiffer Library. The first of these addressed was Middleton Hall of Nursing, dedicated in October 1971, though the push for continued physical campus growth lost some momentum as the college was confronted by the

In November 1970, Nobel and Pulitzer prize-winning author Pearl S. Buck became just the second recipient of the distinguished Rhododendron Award, given to native West Virginians who bring distinction to the state or who are exemplary leaders on behalf of the college.

fiscal realities of its earlier zealous expansion. A 1968 report by the University Senate of the Methodist Church reinforced an earlier recommendation by the North Central Association that the college slow its building program.[7] The humanities/communication complex went over budget in 1970 due to a regional labor dispute, and the college was forced to scale back its plans. The trustees instead approved a renovation of Haymond Hall of Science and a more modest wrap-around addition to the library. Both were completed around 1972.

Stanley Martin announced his retirement at the start of the 1971–1972 school year, though his last year was marred by serious injuries he suffered after his car collided with a tractor trailer near Wheeling, West Virginia, in September 1971. Dean Kenneth Plummer served as acting president until Martin returned by March 1972. Despite his administration's accomplishments, Martin lamented what had been left undone. He believed the

Commencement was often held on the front steps of the library from 1961 until the completion of the John D. Rockefeller Physical Education Center in 1974. Members of the faculty are seen here leading the procession in 1969.

remainder of the original Larson and Larson campus master plan could be completed in the 1970s, including extension of the campus mall to the Buckhannon River, construction of a theatre addition to L. L. Loar and Family Memorial Music Building, establishment of a permanent home for the art department, construction of a Greek Row residence complex for fraternities, and the addition of a dedicated alumni house. He was concerned about lingering debt on a number of the new campus buildings and expressed dismay at his sense that the relationship with the United Methodist Church had somehow eroded through his tenure.

Despite these misgivings, Martin successfully oversaw massive growth in student population, from over seven hundred at his arrival to a peak of nearly 1,800 in 1969. The faculty was the largest and best paid it had ever been, while the number of campus buildings had more than doubled. To honor Martin's service and acknowledge his unwavering belief in the value of Christian higher education, the board of trustees named the rear classroom and office section of Wesley Chapel as the Stanley H. Martin Religious Center in 1972. The board further honored him in 1973 by naming him president emeritus. As a search committee was formed and Richard A. Cunningham was named acting president, the college looked forward in rapt anticipation to the successor of arguably the most influential president in the history of the college.

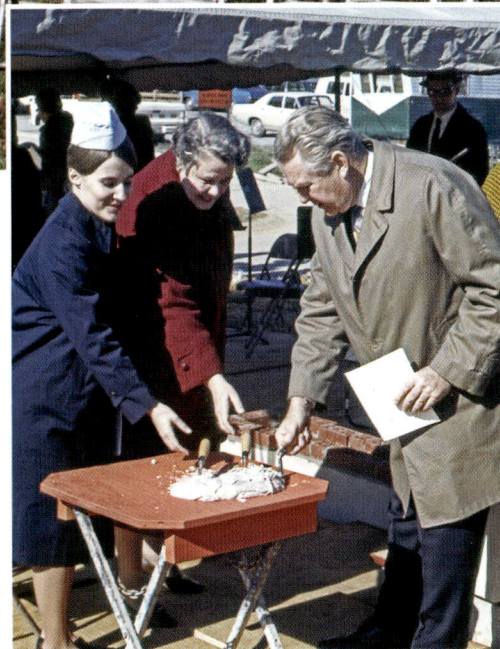

The Western Pennsylvania Conference of the United Methodist Church contributed $250,000 toward the construction of Middleton Hall, which was named in memory of their late bishop W. Vernon Middleton. Student nurses assisted in laying the first bricks in 1971.

Notes

1. "Soccer Team Makes History," *Pharos* (Buckhannon, WV), November 3, 1959, 4.

2. Stanley H. Martin, *President's Report to the Board of Trustees*, October 16, 1959, 2.

3. West Virginia Wesleyan College, *Board of Trustees Minutes*, March 1964.

4. West Virginia Wesleyan College, *Board of Trustees Minutes*, November 1965.

5. "Observance of Moratorium Hits Campus in Group Effort," *Pharos*, (Buckhannon, WV), October 21, 1969, 4–5.

6. West Virginia Wesleyan College, *Board of Trustees Minutes*, May 1970.

7. William O. Nicholls and Ralph W. Decker, *Report of a University Senate Study Committee*, March 22, 1968, 31–34.

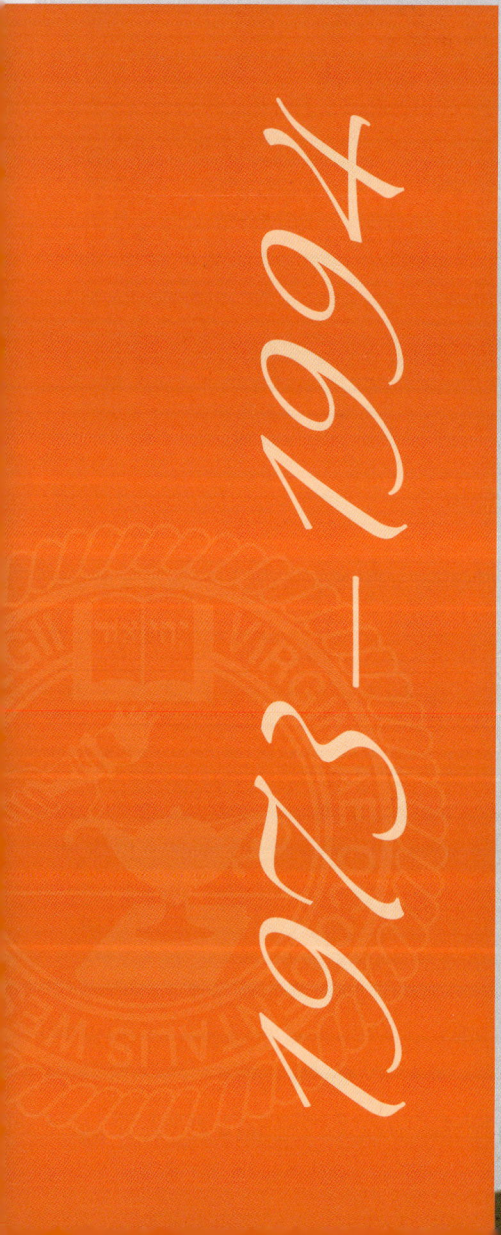

CHAPTER 4

Finding an Identity

The news hit campus like a bombshell: "Jay is President!"[1] The election of John D. Rockefeller IV in December 1972 seemed the perfect way to capitalize on the positive momentum of the preceding years. Stanley Martin was highly respected as an effective administrator, but his more conservative, traditional approach after fifteen years began to seem tired and out of step with the times. Rockefeller's youth, accessibility, commitment to service, and eye toward innovation made him a vastly appealing choice for much of the campus and local community.

The eldest son of philanthropist John D. Rockefeller III and Blanchette Ferry Rockefeller, John D. Rockefeller IV's introduction to West Virginia came through service in the newly created VISTA (Volunteers in Service to America) program. From 1964 to 1966, he worked in Emmons, West Virginia, to improve basic services, educational opportunity, and environmental quality. He was inspired to enter state politics and won a seat in the West Virginia House of Delegates in 1966. A term as West Virginia Secretary of State in 1968 added further political momentum, though it proved insufficient when Rockefeller lost by a surprisingly large margin to Republican Arch Moore Jr. in the 1972 gubernatorial race. Committed to remaining in

Known colloquially as "Jay," John D. Rockefeller IV and his wife Sharon greet guests after arriving on campus in 1973.

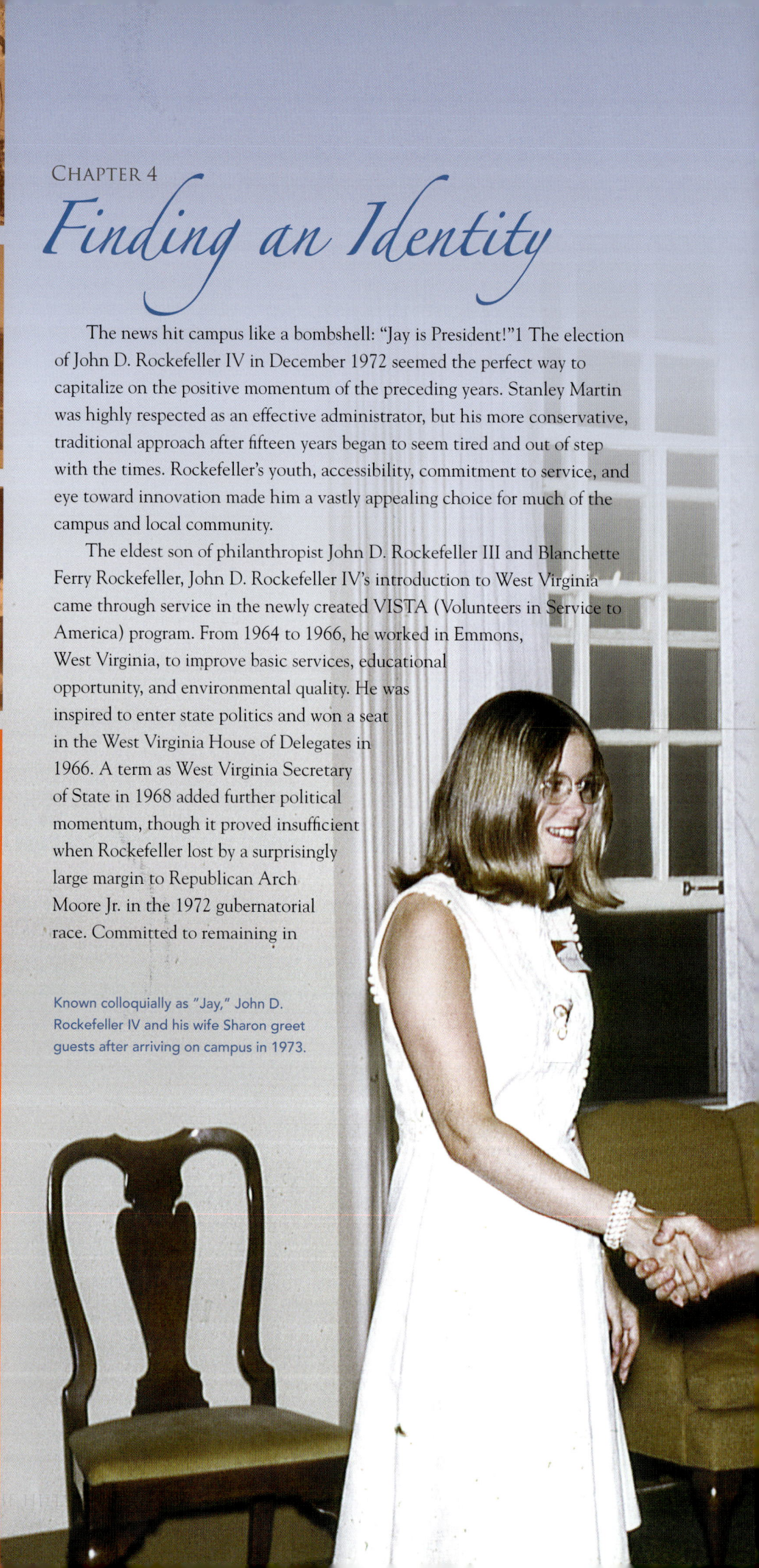

1973–1994

West Virginia, Rockefeller was invited to tour Wesleyan's campus in mid-December, and shortly thereafter the board offered him the presidency, which he accepted on January 5, 1973.[2]

Rockefeller's nine-point plan for the campus included the need to increase enrollment, refine the basic educational mission of Wesleyan to be in step with the times, and streamline the college's management. After reaching a high of nearly 1,800 students in 1969, enrollment dropped off through the end of Stanley Martin's term, creating a financial problem. The national publicity surrounding Rockefeller's election and the addition of staff to the admission office

brought enrollment back to a record 1,800 students in 1976. To improve the college's management, Rockefeller brought new staff into the administrative roles of vice president of financial affairs, vice president for development and public affairs, and director of admission. This infusion of new administrative leadership was matched by the board, which elected an entirely new slate of officers in the spring of 1973, including future Wesleyan president Hugh A. Latimer as chair.

Rockefeller officially began work in March 1973 and quickly implemented a two-year associate degree program in secretarial science in 1973 followed by a new bachelor's degree program in engineering physics in 1974. After

INAUGURATION OF JOHN D. ROCKEFELLER IV

The inauguration of John D. Rockefeller IV was a major event in the life of the college. An "Evening of Music" took place the night before and a commissioned piece for choir and brass composed by Daniel Moe was given its premier. A catered lunch was served in tents along the mall, while a reception in the library and inaugural ball in the campus center social hall capped a full weekend of events.

Top: Nearly 4,500 people gathered in front of Wesley Chapel on September 28, 1973, to witness Rockefeller's inauguration.

Middle: The Rockefeller family gathered prior to the "Evening of Music" for the baptism of Jay and Sharon Rockefeller's son Charles Percy Rockefeller. Bishop D. Frederick Wertz of the West Virginia Annual Conference and Dean of the Chapel Arthur Holmes conducted the service.

Bottom: Members of the platform party included Board Chair Hugh A. Latimer (at podium), John D. Rockefeller, Rockefeller's father and noted philanthropist John D. Rockefeller III, who gave the address (seated in black), and outgoing president Stanley Martin (seated in red).

several years of study, a number of faculty subcommittees also implemented wide-ranging academic recommendations, including an experimental ten-credit-hour humanities core, the introduction of interdisciplinary courses into the general studies program, and the expansion of the Jan-Term offerings. Capitalizing on the historic strength of the education department, Wesleyan's first graduate degree since 1935, a master of arts in teaching, was started by the summer of 1975. Helping to drive many of the academic developments was William Capitan, who was hired

to round out the administration as vice president for academic affairs in 1974.

Another goal of Rockefeller's was the completion of the new physical education complex. The existing gymnasium, built in 1912, had reached such a point of dilapidation that the fire marshal condemned it to very limited use by 1969. Members of the board acknowledged the lack of an adequate physical education

Right: The old gymnasium was razed during the summer of 1974 and some of the bricks were recycled to construct the entry gates to Ross Field, seen in the background.

Below: Construction on the new gymnasium began during Stanley Martin's term, though the Completion Fund continued to raise money until the building was completed in 1974.

facility was negatively impacting new student recruitment, yet there was also strong resistance to incurring additional debt. The compromise reached by Stanley Martin and the board in 1971 stated that construction could begin on the complex once half the funding was in hand with the proviso that no new buildings be constructed "for some time in the future."[3] The gymnasium was officially opened at a ceremony on October 25, 1974, where the cornerstone was also laid. A $250,000 grant from the estate of Stella LaZelle Barnhart, a Fairmont, West Virginia, native and devout Methodist, allowed the college to incorporate the health center into the building as well. The Barnhart Memorial Health Center replaced the old health center located in the house at 68 College Avenue (currently the Upshur Cooperative Parish House).

The completion of the gymnasium closely corresponded with the 1972 adoption of federal Title IX legislation eliminating discrimination on the basis of gender in all educational programs. Legal interpretation over enforcement took nearly three years to settle and colleges and universities were given an additional three years to 1978 to comply. While the legislation was not limited to athletics, it was in this area that it had the greatest repercussions. In 1972, the women's intramural program at Wesleyan was exceptionally strong, but intercollegiate

Wesleyan's cheerleaders, seen here in 1973, have supported Wesleyan athletics since the late 1920s.

competition was nearly non-existent. Wesleyan immediately began adding women's sports teams to move into compliance with the new requirements, starting with women's swimming in 1972–1973. Women's tennis took to the court during the 1974–1975 school year, and a women's track team was added in 1975–1976.

There was always some lingering sense that Rockefeller might not stay at Wesleyan for long. He had been clear during and after the 1972 election that he was not finished with West Virginia politics.[4] In the spirit of transparency, Rockefeller approached the board of trustees in the spring of 1975 to indicate his intention to resign and return to the political arena. Rockefeller intentionally refrained from political work while president, though his interest in the approaching election cycle made such a separation impossible to maintain. His two years of leadership seemed unfortunately short for those encouraged with the college's direction. He and

The women's basketball team took to the court for the first time during the 1974–1975 season, winning two games. Their first WVIAC regular season championship came in 2010.

Students surprised President Rockefeller with a farewell party in 1975 after he announced his intention to leave Wesleyan and run for election as governor of West Virginia.

Under the guidance of professors Charles and Sandra Presar, theatre students frequently traveled the state performing lighthearted, self-written children's theatre plays, such as this 1975 production of *Midnight Magic*.

his wife Sharon made a $250,000 contribution upon their departure in July 1975, which was applied to the Completion Fund raising money for the new gymnasium. The result of the gift, along with Rockefeller's service to the college, was the eventual naming of the gymnasium as the John D. Rockefeller IV Physical Education Center in 1976.

In the wake of Rockefeller's resignation, a search committee was formed to assess candidates based on the criteria of church-relatedness, administrative style, and view toward the liberal arts. The committee submitted Ronald Sleeth (1942) for the presidency and he was elected unanimously. His inauguration took place in the new gymnasium on October 22, 1976, and the

President Ronald Sleeth (1942), a seminary professor, Methodist clergyman, and author, addressed the West Virginia Annual Conference of the United Methodist Church in 1976.

elaborate ceremony included the premier of a piece for choir and brass, "Joy in the Morning," written by Sleeth's wife and prodigious composer of church music, Natalie Sleeth.

Ronald Sleeth's one-year tenure as president would be the shortest in the institution's history and was characterized by numerous complications. Fall enrollment in 1976 missed its goal, compounded by poor year-to-year student retention numbers. The weather turned severely cold during late-fall 1976 into winter 1977. While the college struggled with rising energy costs through Rockefeller's term, a perfect storm of nationwide natural gas shortages and extreme weather led the administration to shorten Jan-Term and close campus for a three-week period. Saturday classes were instituted during the 1977 spring term to make up the missed time. Sleeth also had to carefully navigate the unionization of campus

Long lines were a common sight at the beginning of each semester as students, such as these in 1975, tried to register for classes in the Annie Merner Pfeiffer Library.

maintenance workers, custodians, and housekeeping staff through the end of his term.

The tribulations of the year were countered with some positive notes. The spring of 1977 saw the opening of the new Edna Jenkins Home Economics Cottage, replacing the original cottage on Barbour Street that Jenkins (Sem. 1902) had gifted in 1942. When Jenkins passed away in 1973, a sizeable portion of her estate came to the college, and the board agreed to renovate a house on College Avenue to become the new live-in laboratory for home economics students. Two honor societies also affiliated nationally during Sleeth's term: Mortar Board in 1976 and Phi Kappa Phi in 1977.

President Sleeth resigned in June 1977, stating that "this year I have learned who I am, and who I am not, and basically, I am a teacher, a preacher, and a writer."[5] His departure struck a blow to campus morale, with students concerned about the frequent turnover in presidential leadership. Recognizing the need to quickly restore confidence, the board elected Fred Harris as president by October of 1977. Harris had been a finalist for the job when Rockefeller was elected, but instead went to work for the United Methodist Board of Higher Education. Coming to campus with a Church connection and substantial experience in higher education, Harris quickly set his agenda to realign the management of the college. Instrumental in this process was a $1 million federal Title III grant that extended from 1975 through 1981. The Advanced Institutional Development Program (AIDP) made provision for upgrading the administrative computer system, having also the unintended benefit of creating infrastructure for a computer science major by 1977. The AIDP

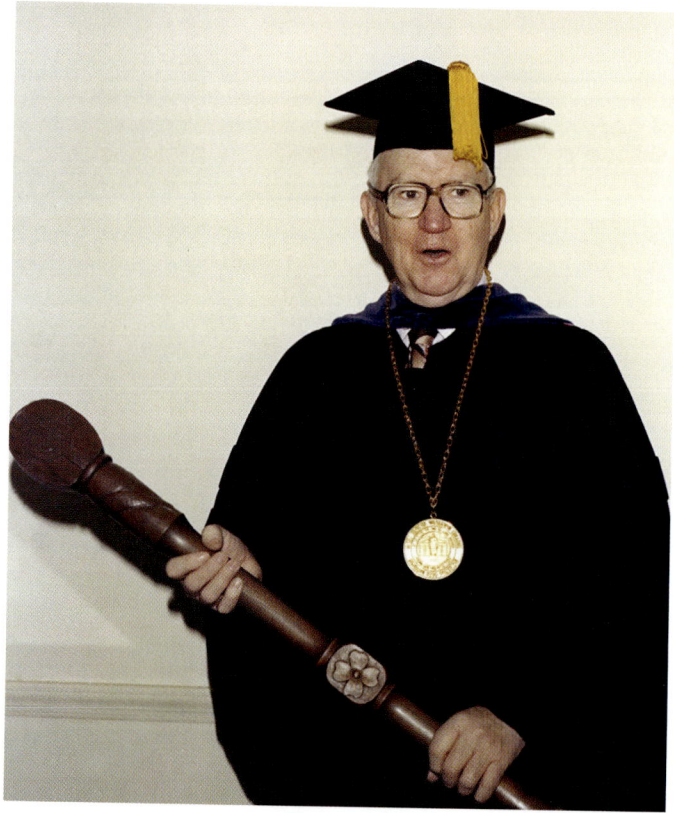

President Fred Harris is seen holding the college mace, which was donated by Dean of Students Richard A. Cunningham in 1976 and used for the first time at the inauguration of Ronald Sleeth.

grant provided financial aid for Appalachian students, funding for curriculum development in the areas of rural sociology and Appalachian issues, and opportunities for faculty professional development, travel, and research.

Aware of changing trends among the college's traditional demographic, Harris made life-long learning a hallmark of his presidency and a specialized niche of the college. In 1978, he proposed a unique model that conceptualized Wesleyan as four separate colleges, each serving different demographics. College I comprised the traditional on-campus eighteen to twenty-six-year-old population. College II involved extension education using correspondence courses for working professionals age twenty-six to forty-five. College III focused on adult learners over the age of forty-five. College IV was not age-specific, but instead encouraged continuing education specifically among Wesleyan alumni.

College II dovetailed with the AIDP grant's focus on education in the Appalachian region. Wesleyan became a national leader in correspondence education through the creation of the Educational Media Service (E.M.S.) to coordinate outreach. Starting with educational programming using the college's radio station, the E.M.S. eventually moved to taped faculty lectures which, along with assignments and supplementary materials, were sent to regional students by mail.

Harris's proposal for College III, which involved the establishment of a satellite campus at the Port Charlotte Cultural Center in Florida, received board approval in October 1978. Wesleyan's relationship to Florida extended back to Ronald Sleeth's presidency. During the hard winter of 1976–1977, the administration anticipated further problems and proactively closed campus from Christmas break 1977 through February 1, 1978, in an attempt to conserve energy and cut down on costs. Rather than eliminate Jan-Term entirely, an ingenious solution was devised: under the direction of librarian Keith Burns, nearly 130 students, fifteen faculty, and five staff members traveled to the campuses of Florida Atlantic University and the College of Boca Raton for classes. The college repeated the experience with 150 students in January 1979, while others opted for domestic and international travel opportunities or took advantage of correspondence courses from home.

College III, known as "Wesleyan in Southwest Florida," was granted provisional licensure in September 1979 and was officially inaugurated in January 1980 under the direction of Wesleyan faculty members Marian McBrair Davis and Sidney Davis. The program took students three years to complete, with life experience credit given in place of a fourth year. Students took six fourteen-hour intensive seminar courses on various topics, leading to a bachelor of liberal studies degree. The first fourteen graduates of the program received their diplomas in Buckhannon at commencement in 1983. The program remained relatively small throughout its affiliation with Wesleyan, which was a point of concern for those who felt it disproportionately diverted resources away from the Buckhannon campus. After the North Central Association echoed accreditation concerns about the sustainability of the program

Retired faculty members Sidney Davis and Marian McBrair Davis, at the head of the table, were instrumental in administering the "Wesleyan in Southwest Florida" older adult education program, teaching even after it became part of Florida Southern College in 1986.

The 1978–1979 men's basketball team won the NAIA District 28 championship and made an appearance in the NAIA national championship tournament.

Daniel Pinkham's choral piece *Descent into Hell* was commissioned for the college's ninetieth birthday in 1980. Pinkham conducted Concert Chorale in the premier, with character/solos performed by Caroline Dees (left), Peter Infanger (1977; center), and Larry Parsons (right).

in 1985, and other Florida schools expressed unhappiness with Wesleyan's encroachment into the region, the program was divested to Florida Southern College in 1986.

Meanwhile, the Buckhannon campus continued to thrive. The men's basketball team had a string of successful seasons in the late 1970s and early 1980, while the International Student Organization (ISO) held its first banquet in 1978, a highly popular tradition that introduced the campus to the food, fashion, music, and culture of Wesleyan's international students. The Black Student Alliance was formed in 1972, in part to push for greater racial diversity among the faculty and staff. The group held its first Black Awareness Week in 1975 and Georgia Senator Julian Bond made the first of two high-profile campus appearances as part of the event in March 1979 (the second was in 2007 as president of the NAACP).

President Harris took a conservative stance on physical campus development. A high national inflation rate, rising costs in the areas of food service and energy, and residual debt from Stanley Martin's earlier campus expansion meant the vision for projects such as a performing arts venue, a permanent home for the art department, and a free-standing building for the business department were deferred. Harris's extensive "Green Book" planning document plotted a course that led the college to its one-hundredth birthday in 1990. To lay groundwork for future infrastructure, Harris proposed an ambitious "Centennial Campaign" of $35 million to be completed by the year 2000, eventually reduced to $15 million to be raised by 1985. To build momentum, Harris also declared a "Decade of Celebration" to last from 1980 to 1990, which consisted of lectures, recitals, theatre productions, art shows, and a variety of other cultural events. Having stabilized the college and on good footing to move forward with the campaign, Harris expressed his intention to retire. The board of trustees asked him to stay until his successor was named, and by March 1981, Hugh A. Latimer was elected president.

Latimer was a former executive with Illinois Bell Telephone Company and served on the United Methodist Church Board of Pensions. As previous chair of Wesleyan's board, he was an attractive choice to lead the college through its upcoming campaign. Unfortunately Latimer's presidency suffered, more than anything, from circumstances beyond his control. Enrollment just prior to his election had been very strong and there was a shortage of housing on campus. The board approved

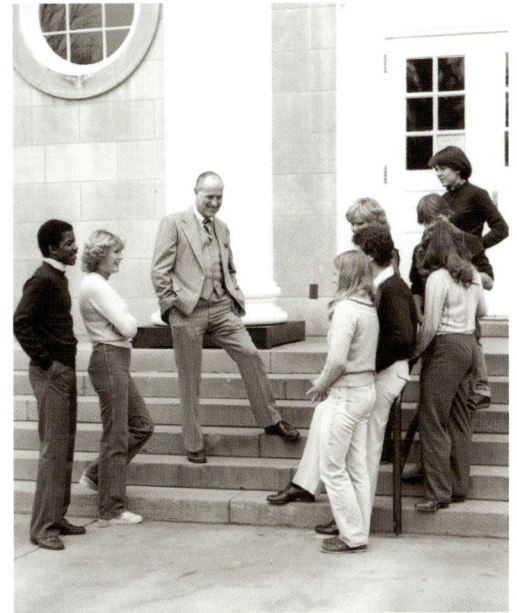

Right: Taking part in the October 1981 groundbreaking for the Camden Residence Complex were (left to right): President Hugh Latimer; Kenneth Welliver, dean of the college; Doug Ritchie (1983), vice president of Community Council; and Patton Nickell Jr. (1956), vice president for administration.

An April 1982 windstorm caused major damage to the partially constructed Camden Residence Complex, putting the project behind schedule.

construction of a three-unit townhouse and apartment-style residence complex on Camden Avenue to be completed by the fall of 1982. The timing for the construction could not have been worse. By the time Latimer took office in June 1981, the United States economy had entered a period of recession partly driven by the lingering energy crisis of the late 1970s. National unemployment numbers spiked and West Virginia was hit particularly hard as the coal industry suffered one of its more notable bust cycles through most of the decade. Cuts to the federal financial aid budget as part of the national program of austerity were most damaging to Wesleyan. As a result, enrollment fell from nearly 1,700 students when Latimer took office to around 1,250 in 1985, and the administration was forced to eliminate some faculty and staff positions.

Despite poor external circumstances, the college benefited from the generosity of its alumni to fill some of the gaps. Former bank executive Mason Crickard (Sem. 1907) passed away in

1981, leaving nearly $2 million to the Greater Kanawha Valley Foundation to administer a scholarship program at Wesleyan. The first class of thirty-eight Mason Crickard Scholars started in 1982 and the number grew to 106 by 1984. The scholarship was a godsend, helping to staunch the massive decline in new student applications due to decreasing financial aid. The Claude Worthington Benedum Foundation also supplemented financial aid funds lost to federal and state cuts, while substantial Mellon and National Endowment for the Humanities supported curricular and faculty development.

Methodist minister Arthur Workman (Acad. 1912; College 1918) made a decision to establish a number of scholarships, as well as to endow the first academic chair at Wesleyan in the religion department in 1981. Workman struggled to afford college, but took an interest in the stock market after he graduated and found he had a knack for making good investments in the wake of the 1929 market crash. Workman's side hobby allowed him to donate over $700,000 by 1983 and the ninety-four-year-old was on hand at baccalaureate that year to see professor J. Peter Bercovitz installed as the first Workman Professor of Religion.

No programs were immune from the unsettled times, including Wesleyan athletics. As early as 1979, Fred Harris proposed a realignment of priorities, asking athletic expenditures not exceed 4 percent of the total college budget and that

Arthur Workman (center) and President Latimer (left) were on hand in 1983 as J. Peter Bercovitz (right) was installed as the first Workman Professor of Religion at baccalaureate.

Former United States President Jimmy Carter, seen here with a number of Mason Crickard Scholars, visited campus and gave the first Mason Crickard lecture in 1985.

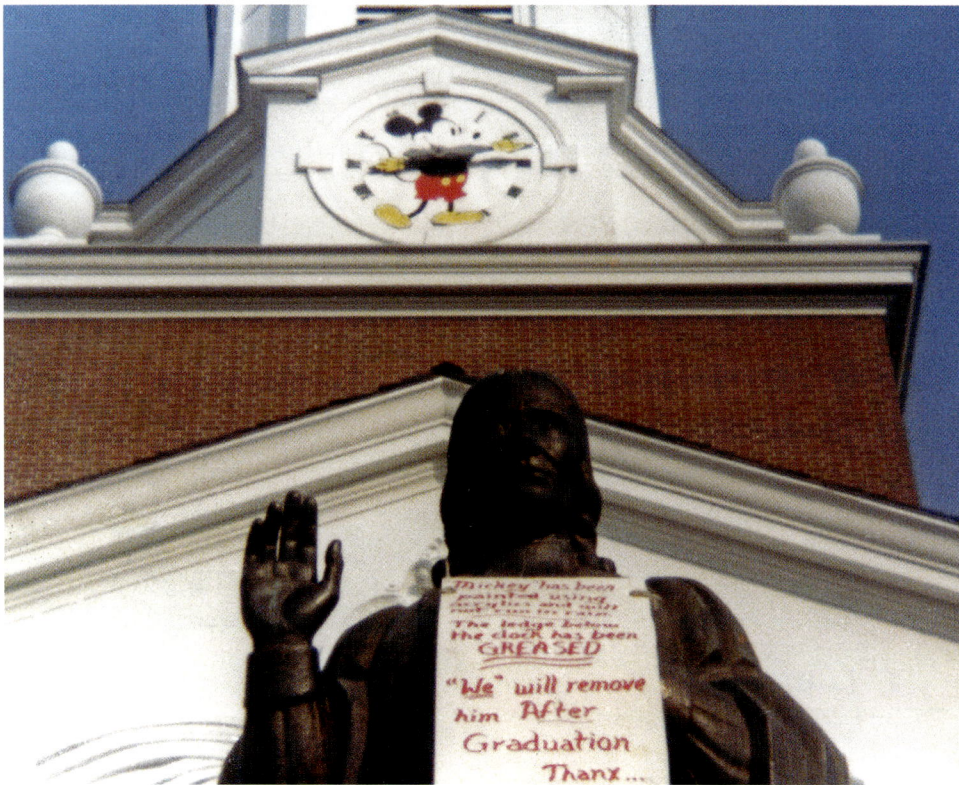

The perpetrators of one of the great pranks of Wesleyan history left the following message in May 1982: "Mickey has been painted in acrylics and will not run in rain. The ledge below the clock has been GREASED. 'We' will remove him after graduation. Thanx…"

With the move into the NAIA, certain Wesleyan teams became dominant at the regional and national levels. The men's soccer team captured all but three WVIAC regular season championships during the 1980s, and most notably won back-to-back NAIA national championships in 1984 and 1985. The men's basketball team remained strong through the mid-1980s, including an impressive NAIA national championship run in 1982–1983. The women's tennis team won their first ever WVIAC championship in 1982, while the women's track team won conference titles in 1980, 1983, and 1984.

Though enrollment struggled through much of Latimer's presidency, the college remained willing to experiment with new ways to bring students to campus by capitalizing on areas of academic strength. The education department added a second graduate program in 1984, the master of education, which was specifically geared to existing educators with undergraduate degrees in the field. A summer gifted camp for younger students started in

football become a National Collegiate Athletic Association (NCAA) Division III sport, while all other sports remain in Division II. Though this did not come to pass, a board-appointed Committee on Athletics in October 1981 recommended Wesleyan leave the NCAA and align with the NAIA (National Association of Intercollegiate Athletics), which represented smaller collegiate athletic programs. Most controversially, the committee recommended the entire football program be eliminated, though the board rejected the proposal. A decision was made to follow the majority of WVIAC schools into the NAIA, while retaining affiliate status in the NCAA.

Phyllis Kohl Coston (1953; Hon. 1998) created the Special Support Services Program as an extension of the Learning Center in 1982 to help students with dyslexia and other mild to moderate learning disabilities succeed in a college environment.

1983, spearheaded by physics professor Joseph Wiest. Wesleyan also hosted the first West Virginia Governor's Honors Academy in the summer of 1984, a program initiated by then-Governor John D. Rockefeller IV, which brought 150 exceptional high school students to campus during July to take courses in a variety of subjects.

Hugh Latimer's final year in office in 1985 proved to be an eventful one, with the deaths of former presidents Stanley Martin in January and Ronald Sleeth in April. In early November, mere days after Latimer announced his intention to retire at the end of the 1985–1986 school year, heavy rains led to cataclysmic flooding throughout much of West Virginia. Buckhannon was luckier than many towns in the region and, despite the loss of power, water, and telephone service to campus, student organizations mobilized to help flood victims in the community. The chapel office became a dispatch center, collecting cleaning supplies and arranging transportation, while the college also hosted students from Marshall University who came to assist in the cleanup efforts.

When the Buckhannon River overflowed its banks in November 1985, students were unexpectedly forced to evacuate the Camden Residence Complex late at night, while the new Kappa Alpha house on College Avenue was inundated.

WESLEYAN PEACE AWARD

Established in 1985, the Wesleyan Peace Award is given to a person, group, or organization in recognition of a significant contribution to the attainment of peace and justice. Winners are chosen by the Wesleyan Peace Education Committee and the award acknowledges attempts to raise social consciousness, create social policy, or establish social programs or organizations that study peaceful techniques for conflict resolution. Recipients include:

Senator Jennings Randolph (1985)
President Jimmy Carter (1985)
The Center for Defense Information (1987)
The United Methodist Council of Bishops (1988)
Ossie Davis (1992)
b.f. maiz (1994)
Julian Bond (2007)

Poet b.f. maiz received the Peace Award in May 1994 for his activism, involvement in the civil rights movement, and work as an educator.

As Latimer departed campus in the spring of 1986, the board whittled down its large pool of presidential applicants to one man, Thomas B. Courtice. Having served as president of Westbrook College in Maine, Courtice brought administrative experience as well as youth and vigor to the office. Though he wasn't officially inaugurated until October 1987, he dove immediately into the work of helping the college with its continued recovery. New student enrollment started increasing in 1987 and the trend continued through much of Courtice's term. The first few years were not easy, though conservative budgeting and strategic program evaluation gave the college the foothold it needed to regain financial control and add students.

One such example was the earlier addition of the master of business administration degree in 1986, which originally catered to working professionals in the region. The program thrived because it offered evening classes and summer sessions to accommodate non-traditional students, though it quickly became popular with traditional undergraduate students as well. At the same time, a precipitous drop-off in nursing students triggered a program review that nearly resulted in the department's discontinuation. With some restructuring and aggressive recruitment efforts, the program rebounded

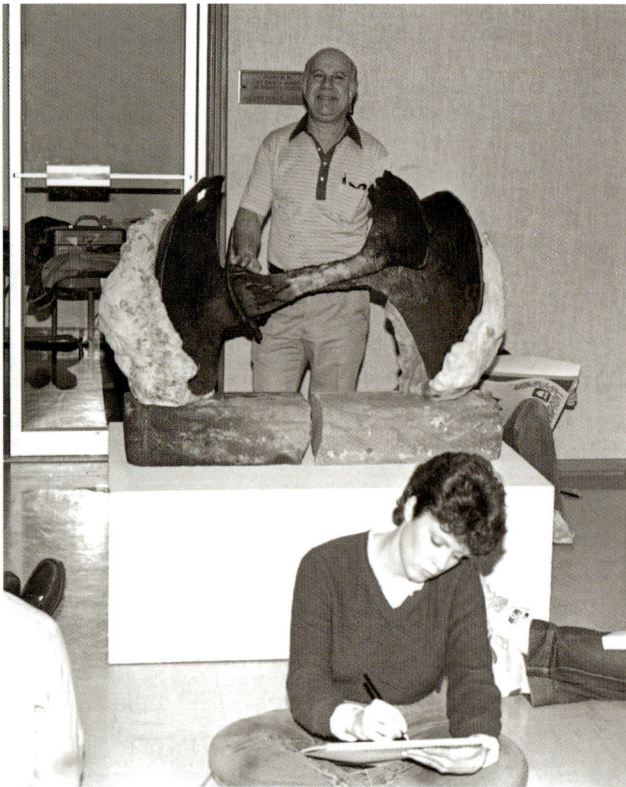

Art professor Stephen Tinelli (standing) is with students in the Sleeth Gallery, first established in the chapel narthex basement in 1977 and named in Ronald Sleeth's memory after his death in 1985.

President Thomas Courtice, an avid drummer, enjoyed playing with the jazz band on occasion. Courtice is joined by alumna and former trustee Olive O'Dell Culpepper (1933) at an alumni event in 1991.

Above: Returning students, residence staff, and Greek letter organizations often help new students carry belongings into their dorms on move-in day at the beginning of the year, as seen here in 1987.

Right: The award-winning adult fitness program, started in the fall of 1983 by professor Robert Braine (left), eventually led the college to add sports medicine and athletic training majors.

healthily. By 1990, the college also began offering a sports medicine major, which emerged from the existing curricular strength in physical education.

The age and condition of the Benson House on Meade Street forced the art department to relocate in 1986, this time to the first two floors of the Annex Building. The lack of a permanent space for the department was a long-acknowledged problem. An attempt was made during Latimer's term to construct a joint art/computer science/business complex, but difficulties identifying an appropriate site and a lack of funding meant the proposal never came to fruition.

Two athletic giants at Wesleyan were honored with sports facilities named for them. In March 1986, the Franklin C. "Hank" Ellis Baseball Field was dedicated to acknowledge the thirty-six-year contribution Ellis (1943) had made to Wesleyan as a faculty member and coach of the basketball, baseball, and cross country teams. The untimely death of Samuel Ross (1952) in 1988 led to the tennis complex being named in his memory. Ross, the son of legendary Wesleyan football coach Cecil B. "Cebe" Ross (1923), grew up around Wesleyan

Sam Ross (1952) and Franklin "Hank" Ellis (1943) both had long and distinguished teaching careers. Additionally, Ross (left) served as athletic director, while Ellis (right) coached baseball, basketball, and cross country.

The men's soccer team dominated through the 1980s, winning five NAIA national championships and prompting campus celebrations, such as the one seen here in the S.C.O.W. in 1989.

athletics and later served as dean of men and as a member of the physical education faculty.

New sports, such as women's volleyball in 1986 and women's soccer in 1989, joined existing men's teams that excelled in NAIA and WVIAC competition. The men's soccer team continued their dominance with three more NAIA national championships in 1989, 1990, and 1994. Women's volleyball won a resounding four straight WVIAC championships starting in 1991, while women's cross country won three consecutive titles starting in 1989. With notable exceptions, the football team struggled through the 1970s and 1980s, and this was only exacerbated by conflicts with the WVIAC about the conference's round-robin scheduling format. The college decided to withdraw completely from the WVIAC in 1986 because of the disagreement, making Wesleyan an NAIA independent school for two years until the rift was repaired in 1988. Coach and faculty member George Klebez (1965) continued his long and successful affiliation with Wesleyan when he was named athletic director in 1992, a position he retained until his retirement in 2008.

Television cable executive C. O. Erickson cuts the ribbon on the new Erickson Alumni Center at a dedication ceremony in May 1992.

As the "Decade of Celebration" drew to a close with the college's centennial in 1990, a four-year "Second Century" campaign with a goal of $23 million was initiated to boost the endowment and procure funding for a new performing arts center and renovations to the Jenkins dining hall. In April 1991, President Courtice was informed of the intention of Parkersburg, West Virginia, native C. O. Erickson to donate $200,000 to establish a dedicated alumni house on campus. Erickson's singular vision to encourage alumni engagement led to the establishment of similar centers at nearly every institution of higher learning in West Virginia. The Benson House, former home of the nursing and art departments, was given new life with a substantial restoration.

Wesleyan's historic orientation toward community service led to new co-curricular developments in the 1990s. For years, outreach was done primarily by student organizations in isolated pockets. The Student Volunteer Band was one of the earliest such organizations, pre-

dating 1910. The Student Service Projects of the mid-1960s involved students in local service, such as the trips to the old Weston State Hospital to provide recreation for patients and work with the Big Brothers, Big Sisters program. Student organizations came together in 1984 for the first

A children's festival, first organized by Wesleyan student volunteers in 1991, drew nearly three hundred young people from the community and became a regular event.

annual "Christmas on Campus" that brought second- and third-grade students to Wesleyan for a variety of events. Service became a more integral part of the campus experience when the college received a two-year, $15,000 grant in 1990 to create a mentorship program with students at French Creek Elementary School. An Office of Volunteer Services was formed to coordinate the grant, along with another $50,000 grant aimed at promoting volunteer involvement in literacy efforts through a 1991 Jan-Term course.

This new wave of community outreach caught the attention of the Princeton, New Jersey-based Corella and Bertram F. Bonner Foundation, which named Wesleyan one of twenty-two institutions to host its new service-based scholarship program in 1992. Bonner Scholars received substantial tuition support and, in turn, were required to complete ten hours of community service per week and an intensive summer service experience during each of their four years. The sixty or more students involved in the program at any given time changed the face

of service at Wesleyan and greatly improved the college's relationship with the surrounding community.

As the "Second Century" campaign gained momentum, a performing arts center was still an objective of the campaign, yet the closure of the McCuskey dining room around 1985, the crowded conditions of the Jenkins dining room, and an aging kitchen facility forced the college to reassess its priorities. As movement began toward construction of a new dining center, President Courtice submitted his resignation in February 1994, having been offered the presidency at Ohio Wesleyan University. Under Courtice's leadership, the college had emerged from the turmoil of the 1980s with a greater sense of identity and purpose. His emphasis on community service and measured growth meant the college was well poised to confidently enter the new millennium.

Notes

1. "Jay is President!" *Pharos* (Buckhannon, WV), January 9, 1973, 1.

2. "Wesleyan Presidency Said Going to Jay Rockefeller," *Raleigh Register*, December 22, 1972, 8. "Presidency of College Accepted by Rockefeller," *Weirton Daily Times*, January 6, 1973, 1.

3. West Virginia Wesleyan College, *Board of Trustees Minutes*, October 1971.

4. Richard Grimes, "Jay Rockefeller Shocked by Size of Moore Margin," *Charleston Daily Mail*, November 8, 1972, 1. "Gov. Moore Scores Stunning Victory," *Weirton Daily Times*, November 8, 1972, 1.

5. "Dr. Harris Receives Symbols of Office," *Sundial*, November 1977, 1.

Rather than renovate the existing Jenkins Hall dining facility, the trustees broke ground in May 1994 on a new dining hall that eventually connected to the Benedum Campus Community Center.

CHAPTER 5

From Good to Great

The steady growth and development restored through Thomas Courtice's presidency greatly boosted the morale and solidified Wesleyan's reputation as a premier liberal arts institution in the region. Attention turned to Courtice's successor, William Haden, who was elected by the board in October of 1994. He outlined some initial goals, including the desire to improve communication between the administration and the campus community, a need to improve outreach to both alumni and the United Methodist Church, and a plan to address ongoing facility needs, specifically a performing arts center to replace the badly aging Atkinson Auditorium.

1995–Present

To clarify objectives and to establish a trajectory, Haden created the President's Commission on the Future of the College in 1995. The group's first major initiative was to overhaul the mission statement. Greater emphasis on internationalization and community service was now reflected alongside historic tenets of a Wesleyan education in the statement's closing line, "…the college aspires to graduate broadly educated men and women who think critically, communicate effectively, act responsibly, and demonstrate their local and world citizenship through service."[1] The commission also identified areas of needed campus growth, including greater focus on technological integration, improvements in library infrastructure and funding, continued development of international and cross-cultural programming, and facility improvements to support the curriculum.

Two major residual projects required completion during Haden's first year in office. Construction on the new dining center was already underway when Haden arrived, and its completion in the summer of 1995 vastly improved efficiency and student satisfaction. The second project addressed the long-deferred

The Virginia Thomas Law Center for the Performing Arts provides students with twenty-first-century accommodations and a substantial increase in stage and workspace.

problem of a permanent home for the art department. The former McCuskey Hall dining room/kitchen was reconfigured in the summer of 1994, turning nearly the entire first floor into classrooms, studios, offices, and a sizeable space that became Sleeth Gallery's second campus location. The facility was completed in 1995, balancing the needs of a traditional art curriculum with state-of-the-art technology to support emerging areas of academic interest, such as graphic design. A substantial renovation of the Benedum Campus Community Center followed in 1996–1997. The first-floor bowling alley was removed and replaced with a game room, campus convenience store, radio station, and office suite. The S.C.O.W. coffee shop on the third floor was overhauled and renamed "The Cat's Claw," while a new office suite and an expanded bookstore occupied most of the second floor.

A 1996 donation toward the new dining center by Upshur County businessman French A. See (1934; right) helped President Haden (left) set the tone for alumni engagement and future fundraising.

A class of ten was the first to be inducted into the athletic hall of fame when it was established in 1994.

After fifty years of service, the old student center building was demolished in 1997. Local alumni came to say farewell, including (left to right): Ellen Roush Nickell (1957), Ron George (1955), Joanne Cadorette Soliday (1969), Alice "Ace" Knox (1949), Richard Ralston (1964), and J. Brooks Jones (1962).

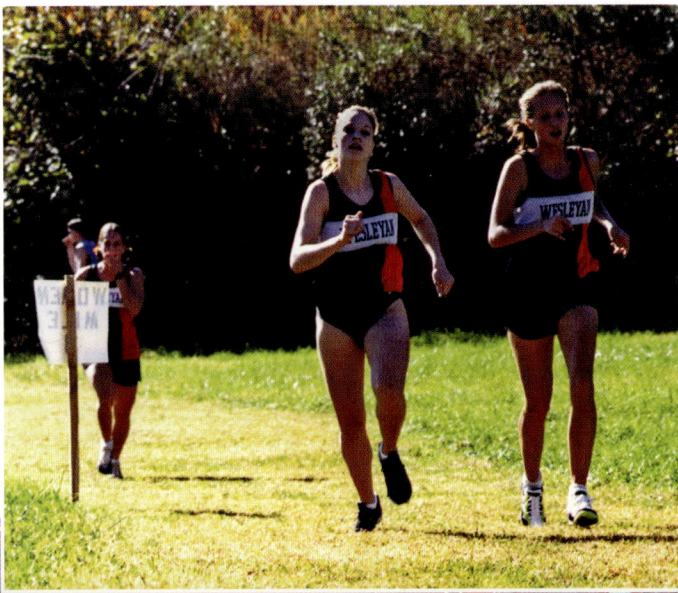

Wesleyan teams continued their conference success after the WVIAC rejoined the NCAA in 1994, especially the men's and women's track and cross country teams. Most notably, the women's cross country team won every WVIAC championship from 1995 to 2009 except one in 2001. The 1997 women's soccer team lost in the final of the NCAA Division II national championship, capping an extraordinary 22-2-1 season. Wesleyan saw two NCAA national championship swimmers during the period, Scott Olson (1998) and Monica Morin (2005), while the football team emerged from a long period of instability with a shared WVIAC conference title in 1995, its first since 1961. Despite the success of student athletes, President Haden tried to temper emphasis on the program, especially as athletic financial aid began consuming an increasing proportion of the budget. Discussions to move the football program to Division III emerged in 1999 and 2004, though they never gained much traction with the trustees.

Left top: Women's softball, seen here in 2001, won all but three WVIAC regular season championships in a twenty-year period between 1992 and 2012.

Left: Since the early 1990s, Wesleyan cross country runners and track athletes have amassed an extraordinary number of conference championships and individual accolades.

Points are awarded for winning Greek Week events, such as the boat race seen here in 1996, as well as for banner decoration and performance at Spring Sing.

EVOLUTION OF GREEK ORGANIZATIONS

Sororities

Alpha Xi Delta (October 1947)
  from Sigma Delta Chi club (local; 1921)
Alpha Gamma Delta (March 1948)
  from Sigma Pi Delta (local; 1926)

Alpha Delta Pi (May 1948)
  from Kappa Phi Omega (local; 1925)
Zeta Tau Alpha (May 1963)
  from Tau Omega Chi club (local; 1961–1962)

Fraternities

Kappa Alpha Order (December 1929)
Alpha Sigma Phi (1946–1961; 1997–present)
  Chi Alpha Tau (local; founded 1923), merged
  into Alpha Kappa Pi (April 1933), merged
  nationally into Alpha Sigma Phi (September
  1946)
Theta Xi (August 1962)
  from Kappa Sigma Kappa (1955)

Theta Chi (1950)
  from Sigma Eta Delta (1925)
Chi Phi (September 1964)
  from Delta Xi (local; 1961)
Phi Sigma Epsilon (1959–1988)
  from Phi Sigma Epsilon (local; 1951), changed
  to Phi Sigma Phi (1988–1989), merged into
  Alpha Sigma Phi (1997)

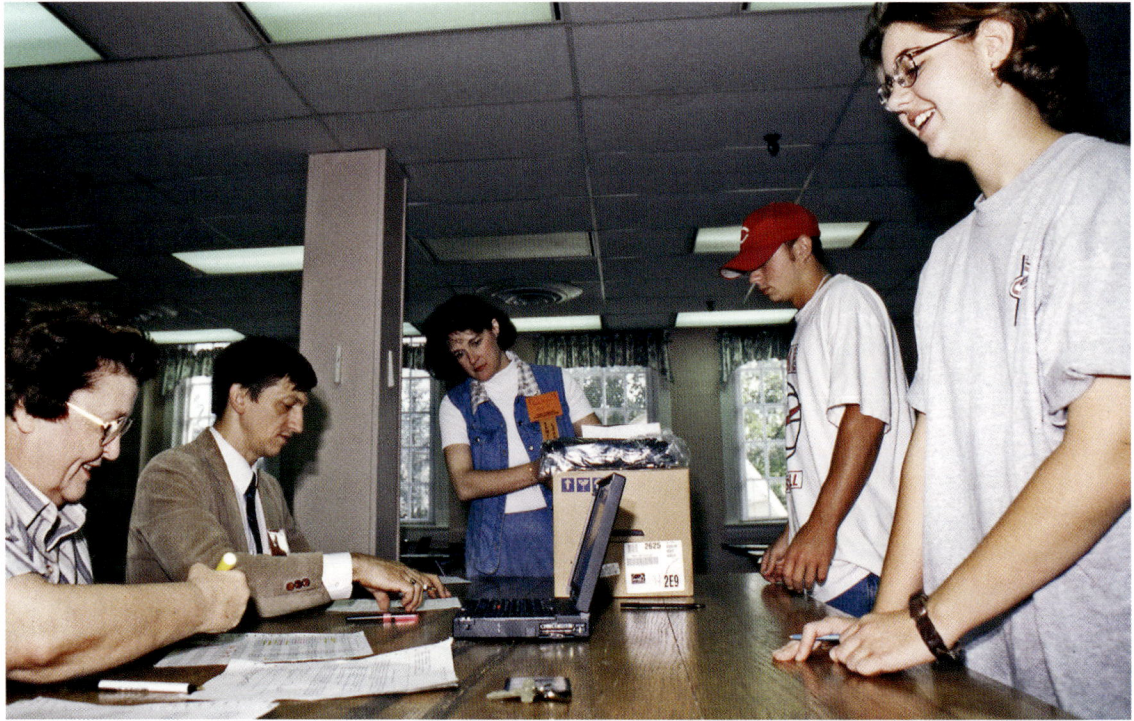

From left to right, volunteer Susan Karickhoff (1955), computer center staff person Tim Loudin, and faculty member Karen Petitto distribute IBM laptops to two of nearly five hundred freshmen during the fall of 1997.

William Haden, a West Virginia native, served as vice president for public affairs at Reed College in Oregon prior to arriving at Wesleyan in February 1995.

By the mid-1990s, computers were no longer exclusively reserved for large research laboratories, businesses, and those rich enough to afford them. There was growing recognition even before President Haden arrived on campus that technology could drive the educational engine of the college. A Computer and Technology Committee proposed over $2 million in infrastructure projects to place Wesleyan at the forefront of technology implementation in 1994. Through a National Science Foundation grant, work began to connect the college to the relatively new innovation of the Internet. Within two years, fiber-optic cables were connected to each building on campus, while every residence hall room was wired with an Ethernet connection in anticipation that student computer access would be vastly increased.

Proponents of the technology program were idealistic regarding its potential impact and were equally ambitious about the scope of what they hoped to see implemented. By the time of Haden's inauguration in the fall of 1995, the board of trustees was already in discussion about models for increasing student computer access. Haden vigorously endorsed the technology emphasis, forming a Strategic Planning Task Force for Technology Innovation and Implementation and bringing the director of computing services directly under the administrative purview of the president's office. By 1996, the sense among both the trustees and the Strategic Planning Task Force was ubiquitous computing, though costly, was the best option to capitalize on the college's earlier network infrastructure investment.

In February 1997, Wesleyan announced it had become an IBM ThinkPad University. The ambitious program between IBM, CompUSA, and Wesleyan provided laptops to every student and faculty member on campus. Faculty received their laptops during the winter of 1997 to allow time to learn the new systems and begin planning educational activities that integrated technology. The freshman class in 1997 was the first to receive laptops, followed by each successive incoming class to spread implementation over four years. A help desk was created in the basement of Haymond Hall of Science to provide technical support, while the IBM agreement specified a periodic exchange of older computers for new ones.

While the new technology program placed Wesleyan leaps and bounds ahead of any regional institution, it was not without its critics. Upper-class students did not receive laptops as the program was implemented and voiced their unhappiness over an emerging digital divide as they were forced to either purchase their own laptops or work during the limited hours of campus computer labs. Faculty also struggled to implement technology in the classroom because of the unequal access to mobile computing.[2] Though these concerns became moot as older students graduated, the estimated $10 million investment over five years had lingering consequences, and some faculty felt the outlay of capital was a gamble too great for an institution of Wesleyan's size.[3] The board acknowledged the program was a calculated, though necessary, risk, and that a larger student body was needed to sustain the program.[4] Despite being one of

Support from the Lyell B. and Patricia A. Clay Foundation allowed the college to establish a music technology lab in 1997 that included keyboards tied into computers containing notation, recording, and music editing software.

Right: Faculty members traveled to Wesleyan's Korean partner schools for a month during the summer of 1997 as part of a Fulbright-Hays Group Study Abroad grant.

Right: Faculty members traveled to Wesleyan's Korean partner schools for a month during the summer of 1997 as part of a Fulbright-Hays Group Study Abroad grant.

Below: Corella Bonner (Hon. 1999; center-front), patroness of the Bonner Scholar program, visited campus a number of times before her death in 2002, including this 1998 visit.

of Yamaha Disklavier pianos that integrated recording and playback technology. In keeping with the initial objective of strengthening library support, Trustee Harvey White made a substantial donation to build upon initial library automation work done in 1993. A.N.N.I.E. Online launched in 1998, making the library's catalog searchable via the Internet, rather than just through fixed terminals in the library. A library homepage was also introduced and became a one-stop-shop for information, incorporating the new catalog with a growing array of electronic databases.

only thirty-five campuses in the United States with ubiquitous computing, the laptop program never yielded the dramatic enrollment growth many thought possible.[5] Even in years when the college met its admission goals, expenses of the technology program led to budget overruns.

In some academic areas, the new technology emphasis yielded exciting results. A relationship between the music department and the Lyell B. and Patricia A. Clay Foundation of Charleston, West Virginia, led to a grant to install a number

Technology was not the sole focus of campus development, as Haden was also a strong proponent of international relations. The college had formed reciprocal agreements with three Korean universities during President Courtice's term, and Haden traveled extensively to cultivate these relationships and develop new ones. By 1997, the college offered more international travel trips during Jan-Term than it had in its history.

On-campus curricular changes were driven in large part by Richard G. Weeks Jr., who replaced G. Thomas Mann as vice president for academic affairs in 1998 when Mann left to become president of Davis and Elkins College. Coming to Wesleyan with the intent of breaking down departmental silos and improving students' writing and interpersonal communication skills, one of Weeks's major initiatives was a substantial curriculum overhaul. The proposed "Responsibility and Freedom" curriculum met faculty resistance and was not implemented, though smaller changes were realized. The sports medicine major became athletic training in 1998 and the dramatic arts and communication department split into two separate units in 2000. Both a criminal justice major and a dance minor were added in that same year. Prior to Weeks's arrival, one of the oldest majors on campus, home economics, was phased out beginning in 1996. The program had been in existence since 1916, but declined through the late 1980s in response to changing trends; its last students graduated in 2000.

In a risky endeavor, Wesleyan became the first undergraduate institution in the country to require incoming students to complete an online application for admission starting in 2000.[6] Though the decision received substantial national publicity for its intrepidity, it quickly became apparent the move was premature for many prospective students. New student applications declined markedly and enrollment numbers missed their targets through the early 2000s, despite added support from the West Virginia PROMISE scholarship program. Funded by the state legislature in 2001, the program provided students substantial tuition assistance at a level comparable to full tuition cost at state schools.

Students and campus organizations participated in a spirit walk to help kick off the $40 million capital campaign in October 2000.

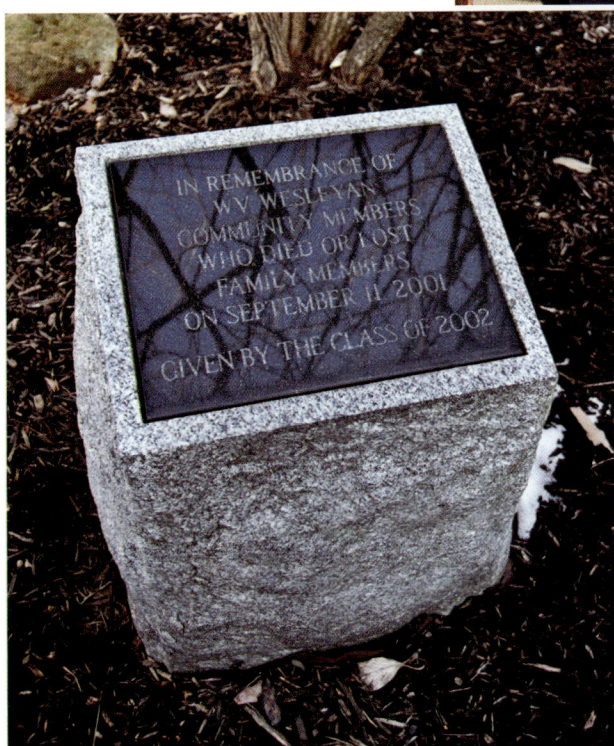

On the one-year anniversary of the September 11, 2001, attacks, the seminary bell in the chapel was rung at the time of each plane crash. The 2002 senior class gift was a memorial stone placed in the garden behind Martin Religious Center.

Faculty members Devon McNamara, William Mahoney, Bess Park Reynolds, and Carol Pelletier led a group of Wesleyan students to Ireland during May Term 2004.

Despite enrollment struggles, President Haden was committed to advancing the college's physical development, specifically the performing arts center promised since at least the 1980s. To that end, a high-profile capital campaign with a goal of $40 million in gifts, pledges, and estates was launched in 2000, and a lead gift to name the performing arts center was received from John Law (1940) in memory of his wife, Virginia Thomas Law. The cost of the building was originally estimated to be $5 million in 2000. While the fundraising effort advanced steadily at first, construction costs escalated more steeply than anticipated, reaching $7.5 million by 2003. Hoping to have most funding in hand prior to the start of construction, a symbolic groundbreaking was held in October 2004, though a revised estimate of $9 million in April 2005 postponed the start of construction again.

The performing arts center was only one problem facing Haden's administration. The heavy investment in technology and instability in student enrollment caused regular budget deficits that began to compromise the college's effective operation. By 2002, Jan-Term was moved to May to help facilitate international travel and was no longer included in student tuition. Measures to control costs became more draconian, as student employee positions were reduced, departmental budgets were sliced, adjustments were made to retirement and health insurance benefits, and employee compensation was frozen.

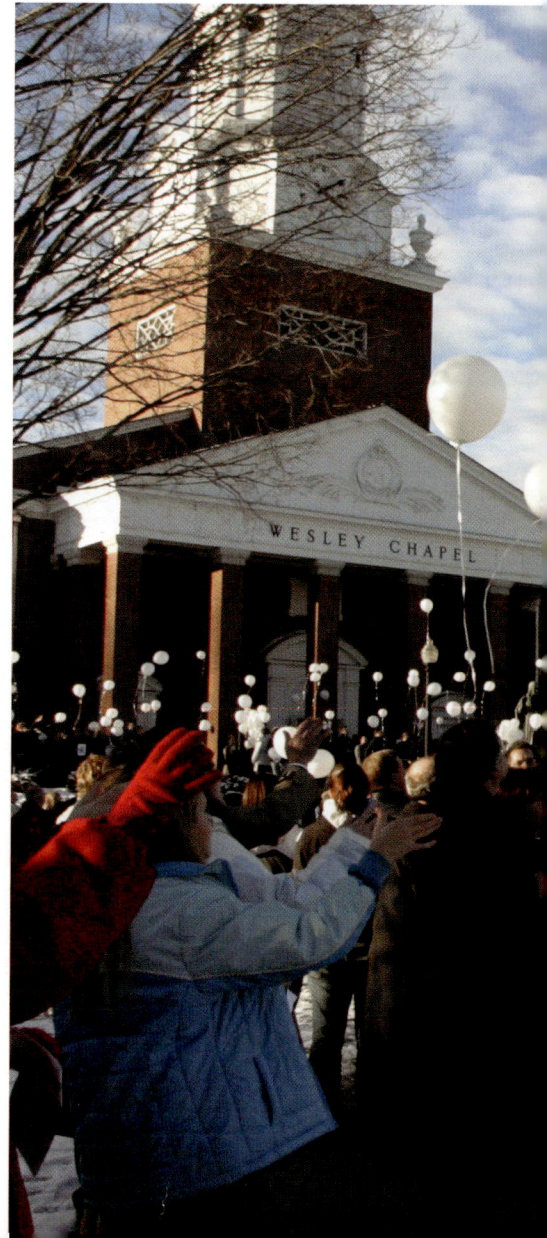

A controversial prioritization process was undertaken during the winter of 2004 that evaluated and ranked all campus units based on their effectiveness, affordability, and student impact. The process provided the board and the administration a platform to allocate resources toward flagship departments, while also giving leverage to make decisions regarding the future of weaker, underperforming, or high-cost areas. The board approved the May 2004 final report, which recommended the finance and nursing majors be eliminated. Haden cited "issues related to cost and our ability to provide the program at a level of quality commensurate with other offerings at the college" as primary reasons for the cuts, though faculty bitterly contested the decision and community outcry was substantial, especially related to the nursing department.[7]

In light of the prioritization process, the relationship between faculty and the administration deteriorated and became openly confrontational. Frustration mounted at perceived overreach in academic decision-making and the inability of the administration to balance the budget through means other than austerity. Two disastrous enrollment cycles in 2004 and 2005 sent the total enrollment plummeting, and the board was forced to declare a financial/

West Virginia Governor Joe Manchin (right) and First Lady Gayle Manchin (left) lit candles and comforted families of the Sago Mine disaster victims during a nationally televised memorial service in Wesley Chapel on January 15, 2006. (Photo courtesy of Brian Bergstrom/Record Delta)

The Upshur County and West Virginia Wesleyan communities came together for a balloon release after the Sago Mine disaster memorial service in January 2006. (Photo courtesy of Brian Bergstrom/Record Delta)

enrollment emergency in November 2005. Haden had announced his intention to retire in the spring of 2006, though the conditions of the emergency declaration mandated the president submit a plan outlining proposals to regain financial control of the institution. The January 2006 recommendations were drastic, calling for staff and faculty reductions; an accelerated phase-out of the nursing program; elimination of the environmental science, math, and physics majors;

merging of other academic departments; and a reduction of some general education requirements to reduce class offerings.[8] Haden's proposals met broad resistance, as the board itself began questioning what type of institution Wesleyan would be in light of some of the cutbacks. Faculty attrition through an early retirement option, coupled with an increased reliance on adjunct and visiting faculty, ameliorated the situation slightly.

The college's struggles were temporarily set aside when, on January 2, 2006, an explosion at a coal mine in Sago, West Virginia, about six miles south of campus, shook the entire Upshur County community. When it was determined twelve of the thirteen miners who had been trapped in the explosion had perished, Wesleyan served as a gathering site for families to identify the bodies of loved ones. Students returned to campus from Christmas break by the time a large January 15 memorial service was nationally televised from Wesley

Having previously served as president at Mayville State University (North Dakota) and in administrative roles at Bethany College (West Virginia), San Diego State University, and in the California State University system, Pamela Balch was elected Wesleyan's eighteenth and first female president in 2006.

The nursing pinning ceremony took on added meaning for the class of 2009, which was to be the last class of Wesleyan nurses until President Balch reinstated the program.

A large crowd, including retired theatre professors Charles I. Presar, Sandra Presar, and Larry Reed (1970), were on hand for the April 3, 2009, ribbon cutting for the Virginia Thomas Law Center for the Performing Arts, which opened that night to a gala performance of the musical *Gypsy*.

Chapel. The college offered dependents of the mine disaster victims full-tuition scholarships to attend Wesleyan. Students and faculty conducted mine safety and accident research as part of a unique service learning course developed in the immediate aftermath of the disaster, with the final report submitted to the governor and other pertinent mine safety and health officials. Through the spring, Wesleyan also hosted joint federal-state hearings into the cause of the disaster.

In February 2006, the board elected former Wesleyan faculty member Pamela Balch (1971) as the next president of Wesleyan. She faced the herculean task of moving Wesleyan toward financial stability, while also restoring trust in the college's administration. By the summer of 2006, Balch initiated a series of campus

think tanks to solicit broad input on how to confront the challenges facing the college. One acute issue that persisted into her first year was declining enrollment. Another small incoming class in 2006 led to a total student body of 1,178 students, the smallest since 1959. Responding to overwhelming negative sentiment from students, faculty, alumni, and local community members regarding the decision to close the nursing department, one of Balch's first acts was a proposal approved by the board in October 2006 that reinstated the program.

Balch also recognized that stalled progress on the Virginia Thomas Law Center for the Performing Arts was a drag on morale, undercutting the college's credibility with donors who had contributed to the project since the early 2000s. As the construction cost climbed

Theatre students staged a 2012 update of *Antigone* in the Culpepper Auditorium of the Virginia Thomas Law Center for the Performing Arts. The auditorium was named due to the generosity of Marvin Culpepper (1951; Hon. 2006) and C. Elaine Karnes Culpepper (1954; Hon. 2006).

Irene McKinney (1967) served as a member of the English faculty for twenty-two years and was instrumental in starting the low-residency master of fine arts in creative writing program. (Photo courtesy of Doug Van Gundy)

to over $11 million in 2007, two members of the board, along with Balch, renegotiated the architectural design of the facility to bring costs closer in line with the original 2003 cost estimate. Construction officially began in the spring of 2007 and the first debt-free facility was completed by 2008. The new space was a tremendous improvement over Atkinson Auditorium, which was never designed exclusively as a theatre. The new facility's curriculum-enhancing accommodations included a construction shop, an advanced theatrical rigging system, state-of-the-art sound and light boards, and a costume laboratory.

Rather than cutting programs, new curricular developments, including the addition of graduate programs, were encouraged as a way of boosting

The first cohort of MFA students, pictured here with faculty during a summer on-campus residency, enrolled in 2011 and graduated in 2013.

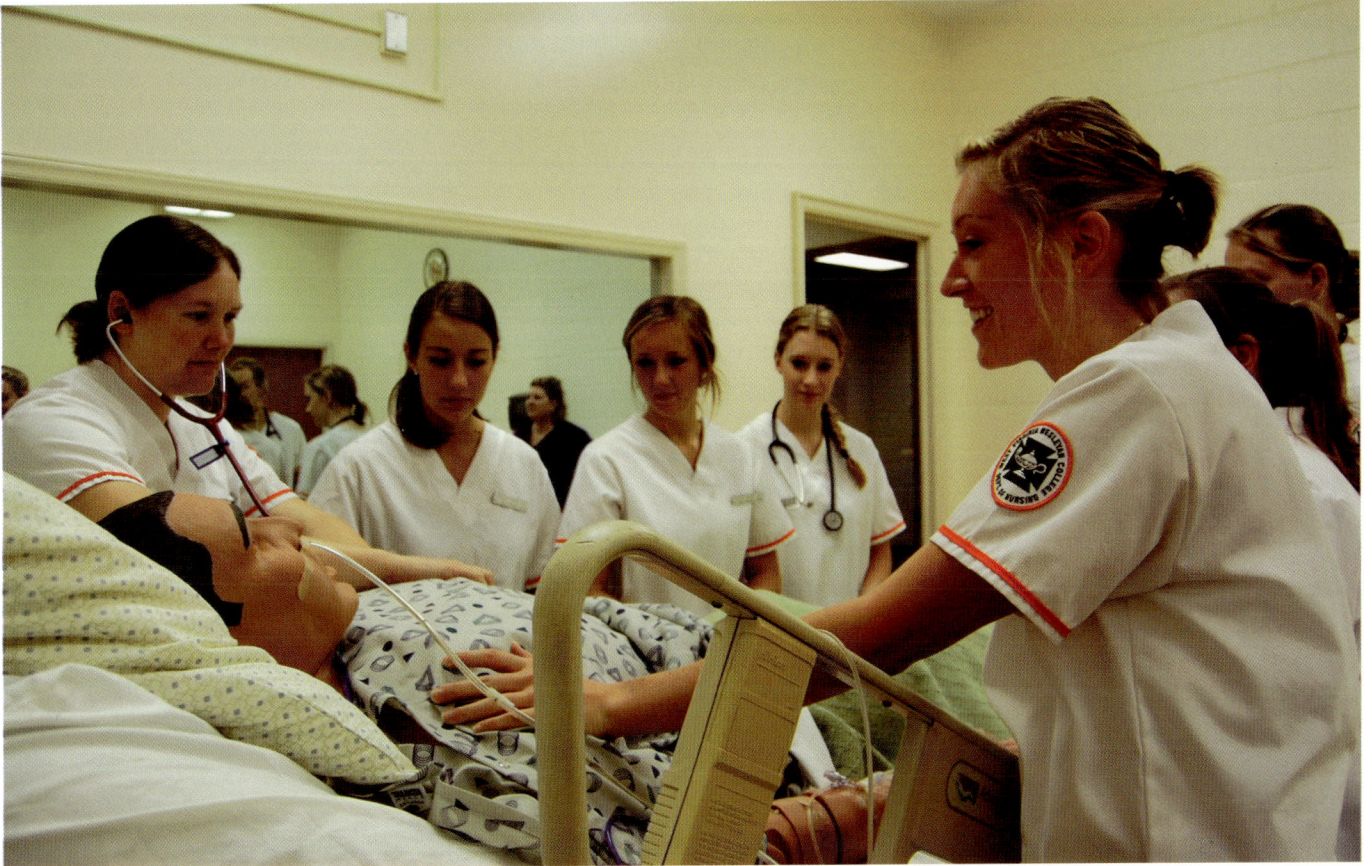

The Naylor Family Foundation provided funding to renovate the nursing simulation laboratory and provide state-of-the-art manikins that reproduce various clinical conditions and react realistically to the care administered by student nurses.

student enrollment. In 2007, the education department revived the master of education degree that had been phased out in 1993, and new graduate programs in athletic training and nursing followed shortly thereafter. West Virginia Poet Laureate and faculty member Irene McKinney (1967) gave voice and vision to a new low-residency master of fine arts (MFA) program in creative writing in 2011. The strength of the English department brought major names in the literary world to campus to participate in the program's regular on-campus residencies. After McKinney's untimely death in 2012, a teaching fellowship was established in her memory to allow an exceptional MFA student to teach undergraduate courses at Wesleyan while pursuing literary development and gaining professional experience.

New minors in library science and gender studies were approved in 2008, along with a new major in media studies. The popularity of the gender studies program led to its approval as a full major in 2012, and a digital photography major was also added that year. In an effort to solidify assessment efforts and foster collaboration, Dean Larry Parsons implemented one of Stanley Martin's early curricular proposals: an academic structure based around combined schools rather than individual departments. In 2010, Schools of Science, Education, Fine Arts and Humanities, Social and Behavioral Science, Business, Exercise Science and Athletic Training, and Nursing were established. Exercise Science/Athletic Training and Nursing merged into a single School of Health Science in 2012. New interdisciplinary programs emerged from the model, including an undergraduate sport business major started in 2012 and graduate-level collaboration between the nursing and business programs.

Katie Oreskovich Loudin (2007) was named a Fulbright Scholar in 2007, the college's second ever and the first since 1968. Led through the

An anonymous donor provided $3 million to assist Wesleyan with debt reduction, aide in construction of the David E. Reemsnyder Research Center, and establish a campus green space and fountain in front of Wesley Chapel, fulfilling one of the original visions of Stanley Martin's 1962 campus master plan.

Retired English professor John Saunders (far left) poses with Wesleyan's tenth and eleventh Fulbright English teaching assistants (center left to right) Cassie Bodkin (2012) and Kaitlen Whitt (2012) and President Balch (1971) in 2012.

application process by faculty member John Saunders, Loudin spent nearly a year in Thailand as an English teaching fellow after graduation. Twelve more Wesleyan students were named Fulbright Scholars in the years following and Saunders, in addition to assisting these students, encouraged and shepherded numerous others through the writing and interview process for prestigious awards that include the E. Maxine Moose Bruhns (1945) Study Abroad Scholarship, the Harry S. Truman Scholarship, and the Benjamin A. Gilman International Scholarship.

Wesleyan's strong academic reputation, a revamped admission office, and momentum in the area of campus facilities all helped turn the tide of declining enrollment. The economic downturn of 2008 hindered a faster recovery, though a conservative fiscal stance and well-performing endowment allowed the administration to balance the budget in 2007–2008 and in subsequent years. The community service program saw itself reconfigured in light of the financial situation, as the Bonner

Foundation changed the funding model for its Bonner Scholar program starting in 2005. Instead of year-to-year funding, the foundation offered $2.5 million to endow the program if the college matched $2 million in funds. Wesleyan established the Center for Community

Wesleyan student and staff organizers in the Center for Community Engagement hosted three hundred students from sixty-five college campuses during the highly successful "Engaging Our World" conference in 2008. (Photo courtesy of LeeAnn Brown)

Engagement (CCE) in 2006 to coordinate service efforts and community-based learning, along with a new service scholarship program started in 2010. The final class of Bonner Scholars graduated in 2013, and Wesleyan's first Service Scholars graduated in 2014. The CCE restructured its service program around student-led issue/advocacy teams and instituted a leadership development certificate program in 2012.

In the spirit of Stanley Martin, a new campus master plan was prepared, and President Balch embarked on an ambitious program of renovation and construction work as financial conditions improved. The age and configuration of many of the residence halls, while appropriate for the 1950s and 60s, no longer met the expectations of students or conference guests. Fleming Hall, the oldest dormitory on campus aside from Agnes Howard Hall, was gutted and reconfigured into air-conditioned, suite-style rooms that share a bathroom between every two rooms. An elevator was added to improve accessibility and the building opened for occupancy in time for the 2009–2010 school year.

An expansion of Christopher Hall of Science was envisioned as early as 2002 to capitalize on curricular growth in the sciences. West Virginia Senator Robert C. Byrd earmarked federal funds to assist in the construction, which was to be a memorial to David E. Reemsnyder (1930), long-time Wesleyan coach and faculty member. Like the performing arts center, the design of the David E. Reemsnyder Research Center was modified throughout the mid-2000s. The groundbreaking finally took place in May of 2008, and construction took two years. The expansion of laboratory and workspace led to increases in the number of students in traditional science programs, as well as to innovative and marketable new additions to the curriculum in biochemistry, chemical hygiene, and pharmaceutical sciences in conjunction with West Virginia University.

Following the success of the Fleming Hall renovations, a new residence hall on Camden Avenue

The 23,000-square-foot David E. Reemsnyder Research Center was officially dedicated in the spring of 2010, making it the second debt-free construction on the campus after the Virginia Thomas Law Center for the Performing Arts.

David E. Reemsnyder (right) was a teacher of West Virginia Senator Robert C. Byrd (center) during the early 1930s in Raleigh County, West Virginia. Both are seen here during a 1975 campus visit, with Dean William Capitan (left).

with suite-style room configurations was planned. Based on student satisfaction feedback, it was decided to transform the former Jenkins Hall dining room into an expanded wellness center at the same time. Local architect Bryson vanNostrand designed both projects, and the residence hall was intentionally modeled to include architectural features reminiscent of Agnes Howard Hall. Construction on the residence hall began in 2010, and it was ready for occupancy by the fall of 2011. Though it joined the ranks of temporarily unnamed campus buildings known simply as "New Hall," the building was

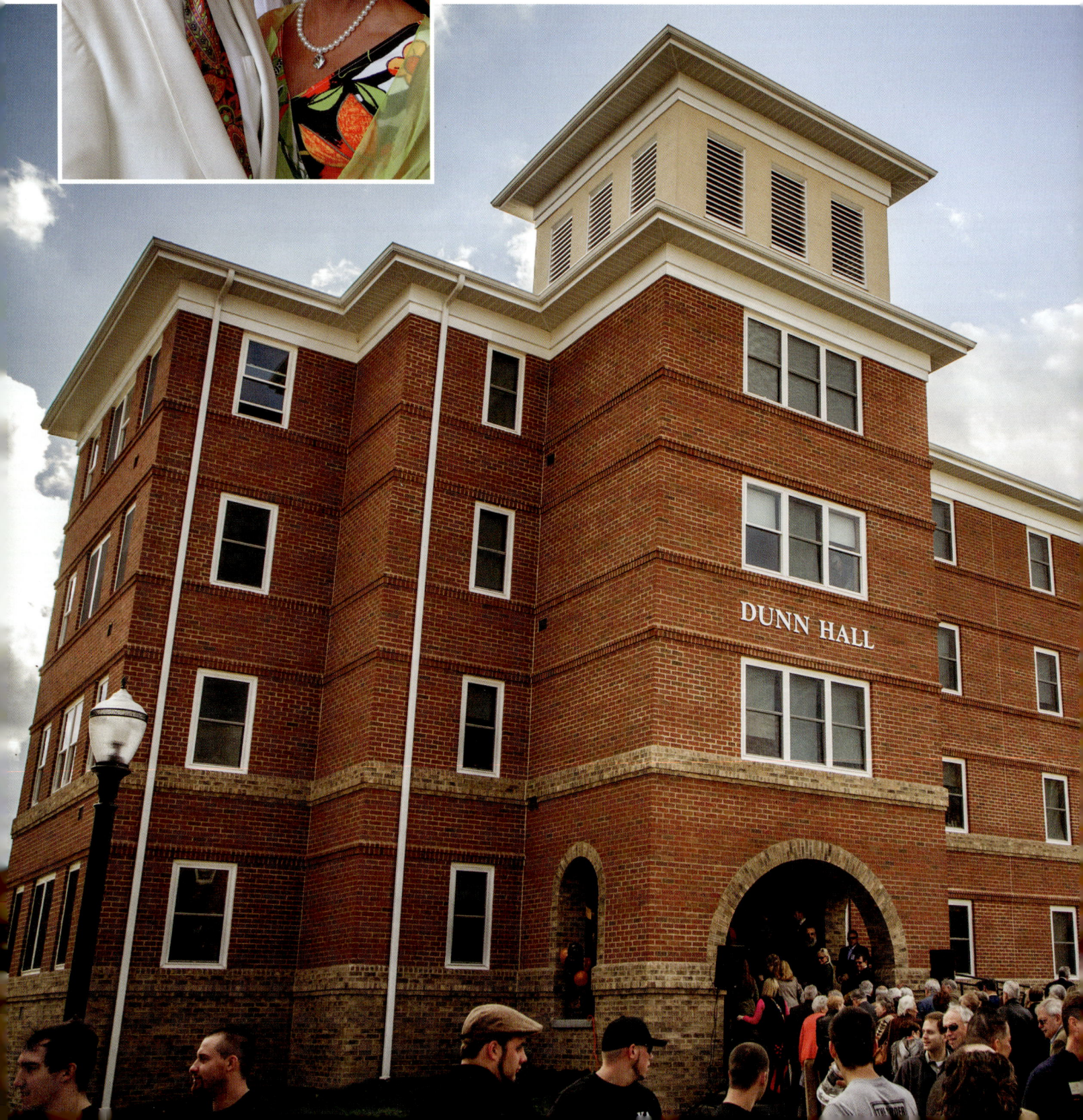

DUNN HALL

ultimately named Dunn Hall in 2012. Upon completion of the residence hall, construction began in Jenkins Hall. The 9,000-square-foot wellness center opened with a ribbon-cutting ceremony in January 2012.

Turmoil within the WVIAC led a majority of schools, including Wesleyan, to create a new athletic organization in 2012. The NCAA officially recognized the Mountain East Conference in early 2013, and the exodus to the new conference led to the dissolution of the WVIAC after eighty-eight years of operation. Wesleyan had been a dominant force in the conference, winning its two major awards, the President's Cup (started in 1993–1994 for highest average score for all sports) eleven of the nineteen years it was awarded and the Commissioner's Cup (started in 1983–1984 with score determined by cumulative season records in all sports) nineteen of its twenty-eight years. The Mountain East Conference maintained the same sports contested in the WVIAC and added new member schools from Virginia and Ohio.

Many of Wesleyan's best traditions remain, while some that were forgotten have

Opposite top: Dunn Hall was named to honor the contributions of former Trustee Thomas B. Dunn (1964) and his wife Carol Campbell Dunn (1963), seen here at Wesleyan's annual gala in 2009.

Left: A ribbon-cutting and naming ceremony for Dunn Hall occurred during Homecoming 2011, with members of the Dunn family in attendance.

Below: The new Jenkins Hall wellness center replaced a much smaller facility that was located on the second floor of the John D. Rockefeller IV Physical Education Center.

Seen here in 1975, former Wesleyan baseball player and long-time coach Randy Tenney (1977) was appointed athletic director in the summer of 2012.

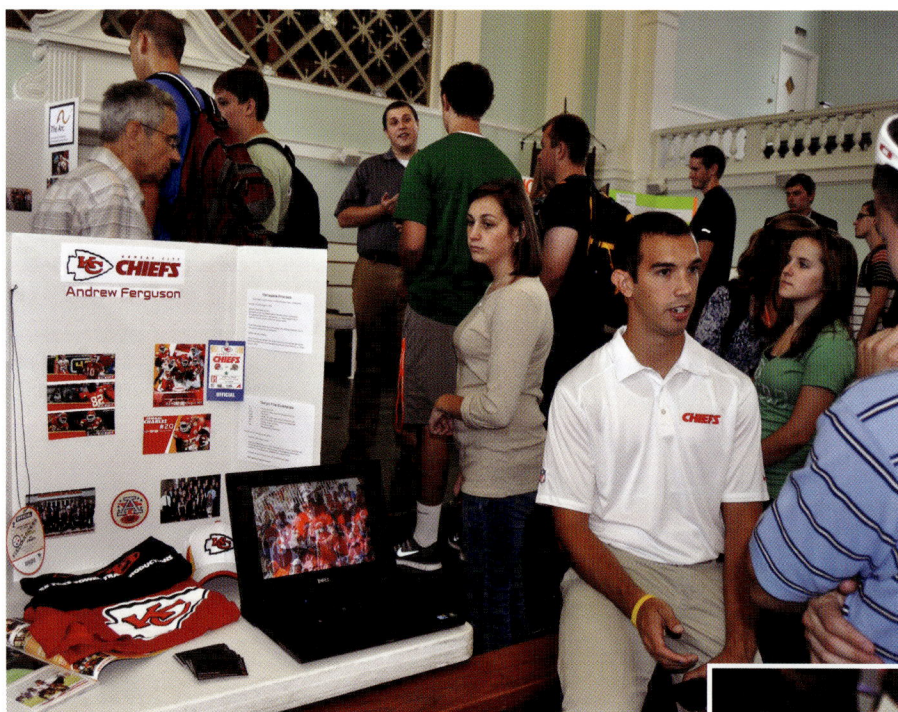

A celebration of student summer accomplishments replaced the Great Gathering opening chapel service in 2013, allowing the campus community to see the success of Wesleyan students in various internship and research opportunities.

William Boyd Grove (left), bishop of the West Virginia Annual Conference from 1980 to 1992, was on hand for the 2012 installation service of Sandra Steiner Ball, the first female bishop of the conference. (Photo courtesy of Adam Cunningham/Communications, West Virginia Annual Conference of the United Methodist Church)

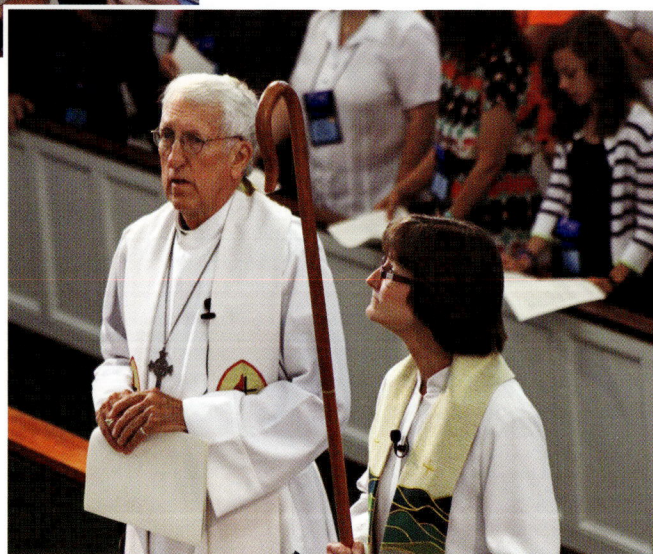

been revived. The marching band, defunct since 1979, returned to the field in 2014. Meanwhile, Wesleyan was selected to host the prestigious West Virginia Governor's School for the Arts, a three-year commitment starting in 2014 that will bring the state's best high school performing and visual artists to campus for an intensive summer learning experience. Alumni and friends continue to generously support academic programs. A naming gift from Thomas H. Albinson II (1976) established the Thomas H. Albinson II School of Business in early 2014 and provided funding for classroom and meeting room renovations and two scholarships. Three new building projects, including the debt-free O'Roark Nordstrom Welcome Center, substantial upgrades to Ross Field, and the renovation of Doney Hall to include air-conditioned single rooms, join other classroom renovations and roof replacements that have enhanced Wesleyan's curricular and co-curricular effectiveness.

From a single building on an empty forty-acre field in 1890, Wesleyan has matured into an idyllic

Constructed in 2014 and located on College Avenue, the O'Roark Nordstrom Welcome Center houses the admission and financial aid offices and serves as a true "front door" for campus visitors.

haven that many describe as their quintessential vision of what a college campus should look like. The community, though much larger today, remains as vibrant as it was when the school was founded. Thousands of students have found a "Home Among the Hills" at Wesleyan and look back fondly on lessons learned, connections made, and goals achieved. In an atmosphere that values academic rigor, diversity, life-long learning, spiritual and religious discovery, and integral service, West Virginia Wesleyan's future is inexorably rooted in its tradition of teaching excellence and a solid curriculum based around the liberal arts. Despite vast changes over the last 125 years, it is this central commitment the college's founders would most certainly recognize and of which they would most heartily approve.

The 2014 addition of artificial turf and a regulation eight-lane track make Ross Field a true multi-purpose complex for football, soccer, lacrosse, track, intramural sports, and the marching band.

Notes

1. President's Commission on the Future of the College, *Final Report on the Work of the President's Commission on the Future of the College* (Buckhannon, WV: West Virginia Wesleyan College, 1997), 3.

2. West Virginia Wesleyan College, *Board of Trustees Minutes*, February 1998 and October 1998.

3. Scott Carlson, "A Small College's Mixed Results with Technology," *Chronicle of Higher Education* 47, no. 27 (2001), A35.

4. "A talk with Bill Watson '58 WVWC's Chairman," *Sundial*, Fall/Early Winter 1997, 9.

5. West Virginia Wesleyan College, *Board of Trustees Minutes*, February 1998.

6. Lisa Guernsey, "A College Leads the Way in Requiring Online Applications," *New York Times*, May 25, 2000, G11. Scot Carlson, "West Virginia Wesleyan Requires Students to Apply Online," *Chronicle of Higher Education* 46, no. 40 (2000), A44

7. William R. Haden, "Setting Priorities for West Virginia Wesleyan College," *Sundial*, Spring/Summer 2004, insert.

8. William R. Haden, *Institutional Plan for Enrollment and Financial Emergency* (Buckhannon, WV: West Virginia Wesleyan College, 2006), 5.

Afterword

For 125 years, West Virginia Wesleyan College has been a place where lives are transformed. Throughout its history, Wesleyan has been blessed with a dedicated and talented faculty and staff that have fostered a challenging, yet supportive atmosphere. The liberal arts core of our academic program has instilled in our alumni the importance of life-long learning while the values of our United Methodist Church roots have influenced graduates to serve their communities and the world.

From the 1950s to 1970s, under the leadership of Dr. Stanley Martin, Wesleyan developed what has become the most picturesque campus in the state of West Virginia. During the last decade, thanks to the support of alumni and friends and outstanding leadership from the board of trustees, we have enhanced the beauty of the school with the addition of the Virginia Thomas Law Center for the Performing Arts, the David E. Reemsnyder Research Center, Dunn Hall, and the O'Roark Nordstrom Welcome Center. At the same time, we have renovated Fleming and Doney Halls, constructed a spacious wellness center in Jenkins Hall, created a new green space and added a spectacular fountain in front of Wesley Chapel, and revamped Ross Field into a multi-purpose athletic and recreational complex. In addition, we have replaced roofs, renovated classrooms, created a wireless campus, established a marching band, and proudly acknowledged our many scholars—Fulbright, Truman, Clinton Global Initiative, George Mitchell, and Newman Civic Fellow.

Today, West Virginia Wesleyan College is well positioned for greatness in the twenty-first century. Our strong reputation, exciting new academic and student-life programs (including many new graduate programs), and splendid campus have made us an attractive option for the next generation of students. Thanks to our steady enrollment growth, careful budgeting, and an upswing in gifts from alumni and friends, our financial position has strengthened.

What will the future bring? Wesleyan must seek to develop new programs that are relevant to today's changing economic climate while continuing to build on the strength of its liberal arts core. The residential nature of the Wesleyan experience will continue to play a key role in developing interpersonal relationships, and the college's emphasis on community engagement and leadership development will teach critical problem-solving skills.

We must always strive for excellence from "Good to Great"—from curriculum and program development to the hiring of faculty and staff. We must make sure we are innovative and relevant. And, we must continue to secure support to preserve the beauty of our campus, while addressing the addition of new facilities to accommodate our growth.

Wesleyan's mission statement is noble and ambitious. It challenges the college to graduate broadly educated men and women who

- Think critically and creatively,
- Communicate effectively,
- Act responsibly, and
- Demonstrate their local and world citizenship through service.

These goals, our rich tradition and history, combined with our vision and commitment to always hold a distinctive position in higher education, will continue to allow our "Home Among the Hills" to flourish for another 125 years.

Dr. Pamela Balch
President
West Virginia Wesleyan College (2006–Present)

Bibliography

BOOKS

Cutright, William Bernard. *A History of Upshur County from its Earliest Exploration and Settlement to the Present Time*. 1907.

Doney, Carl Gregg. *Cheerful Yesterdays and Confident Tomorrows*. (Portland, OR: Binfords & Mort, 1942).

Haught, Thomas. *West Virginia Wesleyan College 1890-1940*. (Buckhannon, WV: West Virginia Wesleyan College Press, 1940).

Haught, Thomas. *West Virginia Wesleyan College The Sixth Decade 1940-1950*. (Buckhannon, WV: West Virginia Wesleyan College Press, 1950).

Kessler, Kent. *Hail West Virginians!* (Parkersburg, WV: Park Press, 1959).

McCuskey, Roy. *All Things Work Together for Good to Those That Love God*. (Buckhannon, WV: West Virginia Wesleyan College Press, 1964).

Plummer, Kenneth. *A History of West Virginia Wesleyan College 1890-1965*. (Buckhannon, WV: West Virginia Wesleyan College Press, 1965).

NEWSPAPER ARTICLES

Braxton Democrat, "Susanne Fisher Makes Metropolitan Opera Debut," January 2, 1936.

Buckhannon Record, "Fire Destroys Tannery Here Wednesday," September 27, 1935.

Grimes, Richard. "Jay Rockefeller Shocked by Size of Moore Margin," *Charleston Daily Mail*, November 8, 1972.

Guernsey, Lisa. "A College Leads the Way in Requiring Online Applications." *New York Times*, May 25, 2000, G11.

Raleigh Register, "Wesleyan Presidency Said Going to Jay Rockefeller," December 22, 1972.

Republican-Delta, "Tannery Goes in Spectacular Blaze; Big Plant's Loss May Reach $200,000," September 26, 1935.

Weirton Daily Times, "Gov. Moore Scores Stunning Victory," November 8, 1972.

Weirton Daily Times, "Presidency of College Accepted by Rockefeller," January 6, 1973.

PERIODICALS

Carlson, Scott, "A Small College's Mixed Results with Technology," *Chronicle of Higher Education* 47, no. 27 (2001).

Carlson, Scott, "West Virginia Wesleyan Requires Students to Apply Online," *Chronicle of Higher Education* 46, no. 40 (2000): A44.

College Bulletin/Sundial Collection, 1909–present.

Goodrich, H. B., R. H. Knapp, and A. W. Boehm, "The Origins of U.S. Scientists," *Scientific American* 185, no. 1 (July 1951): 15–17.

Haden, William R. *Institutional Plan for Financial and Enrollment Emergency*. (Buckhannon, WV: West Virginia Wesleyan College, 2006).

Murmurmontis, 1904–2012.

Nicholls, William O., and Ralph W. Decker. *West Virginia Wesleyan College Report of a University Senate Study Committee*. University Senate: March 22, 1968.

Orangeline, 1991–2003.

Pharos, 1904–present.

President's Commission on the Future of the College. *Final Report on the Work of the President's Commission on the Future of the College*. (Buckhannon, WV: West Virginia Wesleyan College, 1997).

Seminary Collegiate, 1899–1904.

Seminary Herald, 1893–1899.

Trimmer, James M., "W. Va. College to End Segregation," *Christian Century* 66, no. 21 (May 25, 1949): 659.

Wark, Homer E., "The Story of My Life." n.d., West Virginia Wesleyan College President Files, West Virginia Wesleyan College.

Wesleyan University of West Virginia Catalogs, 1903–1906.

West Virginia Conference Seminary Catalogs, 1890–1903.

West Virginia Wesleyan College Alumni Directory Collection, 1909–2013.

West Virginia Wesleyan College Board of Trustee Minutes, 1887–present.

West Virginia Wesleyan College Catalogs, 1906–present.

West Virginia Wesleyan College Office of Alumni Affairs, "Nicholas Hyma Professor of Chemistry 1919-1956." (Buckhannon, WV: West Virginia Wesleyan College, 1956).

West Virginia Wesleyan College Publications and Archival Collections

Index

About the Author

Brett T. Miller, a native of Lancaster, Pennsylvania, graduated from West Virginia Wesleyan College in 2006 with dual degrees in religion and music performance (clarinet). He joined the staff of the Annie Merner Pfeiffer Library as circulation supervisor in 2007. Occasional opportunities to work with college historical materials that had accumulated in the library led Miller to pursue his master of library and information science degree at the University of Pittsburgh, specializing in archives, preservation, and records management. While finishing his final semester of graduate school in the summer of 2011, Miller was selected for the Smithsonian Institution's Christopher B. Cope and Jamie J. Shaw Archival Internship in the Archives Center at the National Museum of American History. Miller returned to Wesleyan and was appointed archivist, coordinator of records management, and music librarian in the fall of 2011. Since that time, he has worked to establish an official archives at Wesleyan and to collect, preserve, organize, and make accessible the historical records of the college.

An avid musician, Miller serves as the organist at First Presbyterian Church in Buckhannon and as instructor of clarinet at Wesleyan. He sings with a number of regional choral ensembles, including ChoralArts of West Virginia and the Madrigal Singers of Clarksburg, and is an officer in the Monongahela Chapter of the American Guild of Organists. Miller also works as the part-time archivist of the West Virginia Annual Conference of the United Methodist Church and is an occasional volunteer at the Upshur County Historical Society.

The Orange Line

I am the Orange Line.
My beginning was long ago.
I have no end.
I am perpetual.
My source is in the West Virginia hills.
My reach embraces the world.
I am in America's small towns.
I am in her great cities.
I cross the seas.
I grow.
I am your warm, enduring memories.
I am your shared experiences.
I am your friends, your teachers.
I am your link to the past.
I am your dreams for the future.
Wherever you are, there too am I.
I am you.
You are me.
We — are the Orange Line.

—Charles K. Dick

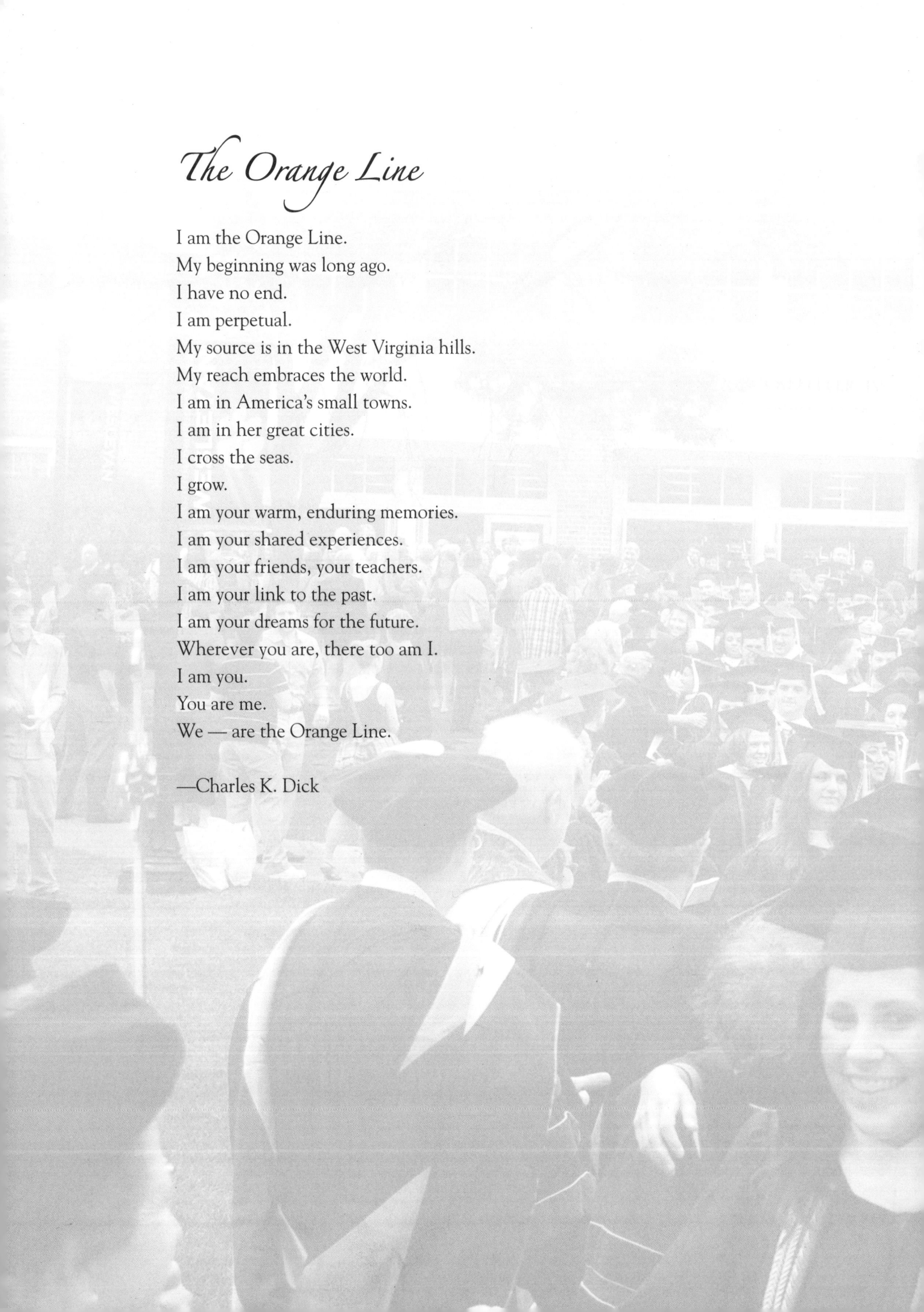